EastEnders

Published by BBC Books
A division of BBC Enterprises Ltd
Woodlands, 80 Wood Lane
London, W12 0TT

First published 1987
© Julia Smith and Tony Holland 1987

ISBN 0 563 20601 2

Designed by Sue Rawkins
For Campbell Rawkins Ltd
2 Barbon Close
London WC1N 3JX

Set, printed and bound in Great Britain
by Butler and Tanner, Ltd, Frome

ALBERTSQUARE 84

EastEnders

The Inside Story...

JULIA SMITH & TONY HOLLAND

With Special Illustrations by
KEITH HARRIS

BBC BOOKS

CONTENTS

T R A I L E R . . .

A familiar TV-theme echoes across the ballroom at the Hilton Hotel. So does applause from the eight hundred distinguished guests who make up the audience. Lunch is over, the tables have been cleared and Terry Wogan has just announced the winner of the Variety Club of Great Britain 'BBC-TV Personality of the Year 1986'. Leslie Grantham makes his way to the podium, trying to reach it before Simon May's theme tune finishes. He collects the award from Lord Delfont then proceeds to a waiting microphone.

'*Lord Delfont, Chief Barker, Ladies and Gentlemen . . .*' Nervously he grips the award, an intricate black and silver sculpture with an engraving in the centre. It reads, 'TO THE ENTIRE CAST AND PRODUCTION TEAM OF EASTENDERS.'

Leslie Grantham, familiar to millions of viewers as Dirty Den, continues his speech, the tension now showing in his voice. '*I accept this award on behalf of everyone who's worked on EastEnders, because we're an ensemble show . . .*'

Back at their table, Leslie's fellow actors, Wendy Richard, Bill Treacher and Susan Tully, look on with a combination of pride and relief, pride at the honour of receiving such an accolade and relief that they don't have to make the speech themselves.

Leslie Grantham returns to the table and places the award in front of Julia Smith. Dubbed by the press 'The Godmother', she is actually the producer, and with Tony Holland, co-deviser of the show. But on this February day, early in 1987, in her mind she is actually miles away, wondering whether her secretary had managed to get plane tickets to Spain where she and Tony are to write a book about the show.

The glittering award on the table brings her back to the present with a bang. She can see herself reflected in the silver heart that is the centrepiece of the award. 'How did we do it?' she asks herself. 'How did we dream up a successful TV soap? How did we create the number one show in Britain? . . . If only Tony were here.'

But Tony is in a smoke-filled, wardrobe-sized office in Shepherds Bush, working with a team of writers on four episodes to be written for next August, seven months away. Tony breaks off to wonder how Julia is getting on at the Hilton. Will EastEnders win an award? More importantly, did Julia manage to get to the hairdressers beforehand?

'What a monster we've created,' muses Tony. 'How on earth did we do it . . . ? It's been hell from start to finish!'

OPENING TITLES

'Of course you're famous now,' people say to us both. 'Rich and famous . . .'

Like most of the things said about ourselves and our programme, EastEnders, that is not the truth. But then, East-Enders has always created confusion where fact and fiction are concerned. Is Albert Square real? Does the London Borough of Walford exist? (A lot of taxi drivers have to think twice!) Is it Leslie Grantham opening that new discotheque or Dirty Den? The trouble with trying to be true to life is that people often end up believing you. In a successful television programme the line between reality and fantasy is frequently a thin one.

We often ask ourselves: 'Is there life after EastEnders?' That is because we have become caught up in the drama too. Walking through a busy street market we'll notice someone behaving just like Pete Beale would. Earwigging a conversation in a pub we wonder what Dot Cotton would have to say on the subject. Eavesdropping on an argument in a crowded supermarket, we imagine Sue and Ali doing the same thing. The characters in EastEnders have become so real for us both that they follow us everywhere we go. Sometimes we wish they would go away, leave us alone, to get on living in the real world, for thirty seconds . . .

But what is the real world? If we believed everything they said about us in the newspapers, EastEnders would be a very different show to the one it is. We thought it was about time you got the truth from the horses' mouths. We are the most qualified after all to know the truth. Here we are in the autumn of 1987 knowing that Den and Angie are back together again, and wondering what on earth to do with them next. Up to now they have told us what to do. Will they continue to do so? The way they talk to us, and take us for a walk, you could be forgiven for thinking that we were characters in EastEnders!

Forgive us therefore, if for the purposes of telling the story of EastEnders from the inside, we join those people behind and in front of the cameras who have made the show what it is.

Julia Smith and Tony Holland, London, 1987

How it was – the spirit of
the East End caught in a
1940 photograph by
George Rodger.

Beating the System

It started when Julia and Tony first met, in September 1971, when Dirty Den wasn't even a gleam in anyone's eye. Julia was already well established in television as a director, with several programme credits to her name, including 'The Newcomers' (another bi-weekly serial, which starred, among others Miss Wendy Richard), 'Doctor Finlay's Casebook' (Script Editor: John Maynard, who is now part of the script-team of EastEnders), 'The Railway Children' and 'Doctor Who'. Tony was working on his very first show as a script-editor, 'Z Cars'. This extraordinarily successful show had already been established for ten years. This was the time of Detective Inspector Goss, Detective Sergeant Stone, PC Skinner, PC Quilley (Douglas Fielding – Detective Sergeant Quick in EastEnders) and PC Render (Allan O'Keefe, Mary's dad!). Z Cars brought Julia and Tony together for the first time and was the start of a working relationship that has lasted (apart from a brief gap in the middle) for sixteen years. They realised right from the start that they had several shared enthusiasms. Firstly a love of popular drama that had the potential to attract large audiences; contemporary, realistic drama with characters and situations that viewers could identify with. They both readily took on the challenge of taking risks and refused to pussyfoot around.

They shared a passionate interest in scripts, and new writers, and a need to confront 'issues' head on, to show things as they are and not as people would like them to be. The 'brief gap in the middle' was when Tony departed the Beeb for Thames Television, based at Teddington. Pressure of work coupled with the fact that they were now working in locations miles apart, forced them to lose touch with each other. While Tony beavered away on programmes such as 'Marked Personal', 'Killers', 'The Life and Death of Penelope' and 'Rooms' for Thames TV, so Julia moved on to direct, and eventually produce the very popular hospital series 'Angels' for the BBC.

'Angels' was a series – that is, one 50-minute episode every week, for approximately thirteen weeks of the year. Julia had felt almost from the beginning that the Student Nurse/Hospital format cried-out to be turned into a serial, that is, an on-going programme, twice-a-week, where characters could be explored and stories pursued in a natural time-scale where they would not be stretched or diluted to fit the 50-minute slot. And, the BBC

Producer Julia Smith – in charge of everything.

eventually agreed to her idea, although limiting her to a maximum thirty-four half-hour episodes per year.

The script/continuity problems on such a complicated programme are vast, requiring a particular type of script-editor and it didn't take her long to realise that the person she needed to be her partner was the bloke she'd lost touch with, Tony Holland. He had left Thames, spent some time working as a barman in a pub and now appeared to have vanished altogether. After frantically combing London, Julia finally tracked him down to the BBC-Radio Script Unit, where he had signed a contract the week before. She invited him to a Chinese lunch and made him a proposition over the crispy duck. 'How would you like to join me, and turn "Angels" into a bi-weekly?' He replied 'yes'.

Five years working together on 'Angels' allowed them to develop their style, fast-moving, gritty and sometimes controversial drama. They emphasised the importance of strong stories born out of believable characters and good writing. At the same time they started to build up a team of writers who have remained loyal to them from that day to this.

Twice during the 'Angels' years, Julia and Tony were asked to prepare feasibility studies into the possibility of increasing the output of the programme from thirty-four episodes to 104. That meant in effect transmitting every single week of the year. At this stage they were not told why. But, on the strength of all the letters they had received, it didn't take them long to work out that the audience wanted one of its favourite shows to stay on the screen all the year round, and not be taken off every Christmas. Both studies produced negative results.

'Angels' was technically too complicated to sustain for twelve months. Even acquiring the medical equipment necessary was hard enough. If 'real' hospitals were finding it difficult to obtain complex medical machinery, what chance did a 'pretend' hospital have? And so, on both occasions, the idea of an extended 'Angels' was shelved. Little did Julia and Tony realise how seriously the senior management at the BBC wanted a successful 'soap'. Little did the 'high-ups' realise how long they'd have to wait. And little did the creators of Heath Green Hospital realise that the task of getting that soap onto the screen would fall to them.

If someone had asked them to come up with an alternative idea to 'Angels' who knows if EastEnders and Albert Square and the

Script-Editor Tony Holland – in charge of all the words.

Queen Vic would have sprung to mind – with Pauline and Arthur, Angie and Den, Lofty and Michelle, Ethel, Dot, and all the other residents of the Borough of Walford, London, E20. And, if that idea had been suggested, who can say if it would have been accepted? Would it have been the wrong time for such a project? Would it have been rejected, never to see the light of day? (Interestingly, two of the most successful households integrated into EastEnders were both previously rejected by the BBC, as separate series ideas, more than five years before.)

Some programmes are more difficult to 'sell' than others. You can spend a couple of years researching a subject and committing it to paper, and it never gets so much as a look-in. Other times you can have the bare bones of an idea in the back of your head, meet the right person at the right time in the right place, utter a few choice words, and you're immediately given the green light. An example of the latter resulted in Julia and Tony having to give up 'Angels'. Graeme McDonald, now Controller of BBC-2, but then Head of Drama Group, was at a BBC Departmental Christmas party, when Julia Smith spoke five words to him:

'*District Nurse. Nerys Hughes. Bicycle.*'

His reply was even briefer:

'*Do it!*'

And they did . . .

'Angels' had been a tiring programme to work on, and they were both starting to feel the strain. 'The District Nurse' was meant to be a rest. A chance to take things easy, and store up some energy for a much bigger challenge ahead. Not that they had any idea at this stage what was in store for them in 18 months' time. 'Go away and play', they were told. And so they reluctantly deserted the staff and patients at Heath Green Hospital and left for Cardiff. But instead of being the 'holiday' they had been led to expect, 'The District Nurse' turned out to be an exhausting slog. A punishing schedule took them up into the mountains one minute and down into the valleys the next, as District Nurse Megan Roberts struggled with the poverty and the problems of south Wales in the 1920s.

On 14 March, 1983, they were summoned to London to the office of the then Head of Series/Serials Department, David Reid. The simple proposition he was to put to them was to change their lives. The BBC had decided that it was time that they had a popular bi-weekly serial. (The expression 'Soap' was frowned upon in those days.) Two episodes a week, fifty-two weeks of the year. It was potentially a massive undertaking. Would Julia and Tony like to take on the project as Producer and Script Editor? It was like being kicked in the stomach and patted on the back at the same time. As life-long campaigners for the virtues of popular drama, however, it was simply an offer they could not refuse, but what exactly would they be taking on?

They left David Reid's office and got the train back to Wales, returning to their colleagues on 'The District Nurse', sworn to silence, unable to tell them that they would soon be deserting them, just as reluctantly as they had deserted the 'Angels'. But people must have been aware that something was brewing, because of the expressions on Julia and Tony's faces. They seemed to have endured some intense pain, as if they had just left the dentist. Yet, why the inane grins?

All they could think about at the time was why? Why did the BBC want to launch a twice-weekly serial, the first since 'The Doctors' which finished in 1971? Was it because the Beeb wanted a valuable nursery-slope for staff training? Or were there political reasons, did it need for example a popular show that featured in the ratings, in order to justify the licence fee? Or, was it simply that the audience demanded it? Being programme makers and not politicians, Julia and Tony could not come up with any ready answers, though they liked to believe that the decision was something to do with a feeling for what people actually wanted.

'Why us?' they kept asking each other. Well – they were going to be a pretty likely choice whatever happened. They knew about the pressures of fast-turn-round television because they had both started in the days before pre-recording when drama was trans-mitted 'live'. True, they had established a reputation as being good organisers, getting their programmes in on time, and on budget, and of encouraging amongst their writers and production teams a feeling of working in a tight-knit, highly motivated 'family'. They were not afraid to stand up for themselves and fight for what they believed in, even if it meant the risk of failure. But failure was not what all this was about. It was about success.

And they had had some of that too. Their initial reaction to the offer had been one of pride – they saw it as a great honour that they should have been singled out to produce the show to which the Sixth Floor attached such great importance! But who else could do it? Given their experience weren't they the only contenders? So, what was all this about a 'great honour'? They fell back to earth with a thump. It was just another job after all. They would do their best and – who knows? – it might have a modest success. It might even do as well as 'Angels'.

So they knew why, why then in particular, and they had a glimmer of just how important a blockbusting soap would be to the BBC. There remained the little question of how?

This little word was to produce some of the largest arguments Julia and Tony have ever witnessed, including several between themselves, stand-up fights that would put even Den and Angie, at their worst, into the shade.

There were basic problems of scheduling to contend with. The bi-weekly was intended to run every week of the year, twice a week. That's fifty-two hours in total, two days and four hours. By dropping 'Angels' and 'Triangle' the Drama Department acquired twenty-nine of those hours. The shortfall was twenty-three hours, less than a single day. That was the amount of extra drama output that would have to be found somewhere in the system if the programme was to get off the ground. And it would have to be found without affecting/upsetting existing shows. Problem number one was how to find the time, the space and the staff.

Before the bureaucrats and the computers took over, the Producer and Script-Editor decided to sit down for five minutes and assess exactly what they had got. It might be the last chance they would have to consider the artistic qualities of the project, before lists, forms, print-outs, memos and money would drag them under forever. And, what had they got? They had a programme to make, and the prospect of lots of hard work. But nobody had a clue as yet as to what the programme would be about, where it was set or who was in it. All they had really got was a frantic search on their hands for a missing twenty-three hours of airtime.

At this point Julia and Tony parted company. After all, she was the producer, he was just the wordsmith. She had to complete her planning before he could even think of commencing his part of the operation. While Tony continued working on 'The District Nurse' in Wales, Julia embarked on a succession of committee-meetings.

Most of the important meetings went on for a period of about seven months until December, 1983. But, when they began, Christmas seemed a long way off ... Easter had only just arrived and departed. The question 'how', had by now led on to the question 'where'? Not where it would be set but rather where could the programme be made? Julia started an extensive tour of Britain visiting almost every regional centre owned by the BBC. Was there sufficient studio space? (She described one studio as being so small that you went in one door and fell out of the other. She was offered a disused aircraft hangar as an alternative!) If the studio space was acceptable, were there ample Outside-Broadcast facilities? Could the studios guarantee regular studio-time, week in, week out? Was there enough storage space? What about rehearsal rooms? Dressing-rooms? How much more time and cash would be involved if staff and artists were travelling to a regional centre from London?

What artists? Waiting in the wings was a group of people desperate to be born. 'Never mind the "how" and "where",' they were whispering, 'we're the ones the punters want to know about!' And throughout the coming months they continued to tap on the shoulders of their creators-to-be ... impatient to be pulling a pint of Churchill's Bitter behind the Queen Vic bar, anxious to do that service-wash at the launderette or serve up a bacon sandwich at Ali's Cafe. But, for the moment, they had to wait like paratroopers heading for a target, ready to go into action as soon as the green light came on, while the technical details were drafted, re-drafted, put through a shredding-machine then sent back to the drawing-board to be drafted all over again. Slowly, a possible work pattern was being devised around an unknown base about an unknown product.

There were fundamental production questions to answer straightaway, such as should it be mainly studio oriented like 'Coronation Street' or all location like 'Brookside'? Or should it be a combination of the two? What about the availability of editing facilities, number of cameras, size of cast, amount of recording time and the budget?

The arguments were starting. Firstly, between Julia and the moneyman, her production associate, Christopher d'Oyly John. How could he possibly work out even vague costings, when he didn't have a clue what the programme was about? The arguments led to reconciliations, then yet more fighting. Rumours were now flying about that the BBC's Director of Resources – Michael Checkland (appointed Director General of the BBC in 1987) – had convinced the Board of Governors to buy the old ATV studios, at Elstree in Hertfordshire, so that the bi-weekly could be produced there and hit the screen in January 1985.

Arguments were temporarily forgotten, frayed tempers put to bed and a truce declared. Work patterns had now been formulated for directors, design, wardrobe, make-up, studio-staff and cameramen. Like the as yet uncreated population of Albert Square, they waited, tongues hanging out, for someone to say: 'On your marks, get set – Go!'

And while yet another committee was formed, The Elstree Steering Committee, so a fresh clue or, perhaps a red-herring was dropped into the unfolding plot. Between the spring and autumn of 1983 someone had commissioned pilot scripts for a possible bi-weekly serial. Several ideas had been whittled down to just two, and the scripts were soon to be available for reading. Julia, along with the other members of the Committee, visited Elstree Studios. It was like a crumbling fairground at the end of a deserted pier, filled with memories of people and past productions long departed. Douglas Fairbanks, Jnr, 'Emergency Ward 10', 'General Hospital' and 'The Muppets'. Would it soon return to life again?

Julia was presented with the pilot scripts of the proposed programme ideas, with strict instructions that *no-one* was to see them apart from her, not even Tony Holland. Julia and Tony were still working on 'The District Nurse' in Wales, sharing a flat in Cathedral Road, Cardiff. Julia would read the pilot scripts at night, hide them during the day under her bedclothes and constantly pressure BBC management for permission to show them to her script-editor. Permission was refused.

The first of the two ideas (about a shopping arcade) Julia liked. But expensive technical considerations rendered it impractical, so it was rejected. Julia was worried about the second idea. Although it was technically possible, the idea was not one that she instantly warmed to. It was decided to commission a second writer to do a different version of the same script. By now, Julia was finding the whole process very frustrating, here they were discussing the rights and wrongs of ideas and scripts and she was forbidden to even talk things over with the one person she had always relied on in such circumstances, her own script-editor. She was being denied the sounding-board she had grown accustomed to over the many years she had worked with Tony. Finally, it was Tony who blew! Were they doing the bi-weekly, or not? If so, then what was the subject matter and location, and where were the scripts? If not, then Tony would be perfectly happy to stay in Cardiff and move onto a different project for BBC Wales. They screamed and shouted at each other half the night, neither quite understanding the difficult situation the other was in, and Tony not realising that the reason for their argument lay under Julia's pillow, all of fifteen feet away.

Now, it was Julia's turn to explode, at the bosses in London. She couldn't continue in this limbo-world any longer. Tony would have to see the scripts. She insisted he see them. If he didn't know what was going on and what it was all about then he'd probably forget the whole thing and work in Cardiff. In which case, Julia would walk off the show, too. It was turning into a parody of a Hollywood backstage musical, with one prima donna after another storming off the set in flurries of talcum-powder. Then, two things happened. Firstly, the Head of Department telephoned Tony in Wales and informed him that he was wanted in London to script-edit a spy series called 'Cold Warrior'. Secondly, Julia was given permission to show him the scripts. She did this, without words, merely throwing the scripts onto his desk, and leaving the room. Tony read the scripts over night. The following morning, he threw them back onto her desk.

'Well, I'm not doing **that***,'* he said.

'Good!' Julia replied. *'Neither am I.'*

They were back on firm ground, which meant that they had stopped fighting, and were in agreement about something.

Basically, there was nothing wrong with the idea that they'd been handed. It was about a mobile-home park, and contained several elements that were interesting and original. But, it had no mileage. Where could it go? Great fun for a one-off, or, at most, a six-part series ... but, fifty-two weeks of the year, that was stretching it wafer thin. The format would surely be exhausted in a couple of months.

Then, in true soap-opera tradition, an off-stage drama occurred. The Head of Department responsible for commissioning the pilot scripts announced that he would shortly be leaving Series and Serials and the BBC. No one had been chosen as his replacement yet, so Julia and Tony decided to play for time, stall, until the new Head of Department had a name. It didn't take long. Jonathan Powell, whizz-kid producer of 'Tinker, Tailor, Soldier, Spy' and 'Smiley's People' was selected as the new Head of Series/Serials, and would take up the post in the new year. Would he turn out to be friend, or foe? For at least a month the cat and mouse game of 'playing for time' continued. When he wanted to talk to them, they were mysteriously busy. When they wanted to talk to him, he was unavoidably detained. A respectful, but unspoken, new tactic had entered the proceedings: don't let's even talk about the bi-weekly until the new regime is in full operation. Overall planning operations proceeded, still with no show, and still with no location, though the purchase of Elstree Studios was thought to be only just around the corner. If the programme was not made at Elstree then Pebble Mill, Birmingham, was the second favourite.

Christmas had come round again. It was a whole year since Julia had uttered those five words to Graeme McDonald that had resulted in 'The District Nurse'. In the following spring that programme would be on the screen and enjoying a pleasant success. In the meantime, it was the usual merry-go-round of departmental parties, an opportunity to gossip with people probably only ever seen once a year. And the gossip was rife, most of it about the new 'soap'.

'*I hear you've got Elstree . . .*'

'*What's the show about . . . ?*'

'*Where does it take place . . . ?*'

'*A little bird tells me you're not happy . . .*'

'*Is it going to be good . . . ?*'

They were careful not to confirm or deny anything. But Julia was sent for by Jonathan Powell – still the heir apparent to Series/Serials – and reprimanded for spreading discontent. Furthermore, she was warned to be 'on her best behaviour' at the farewell lunch for David Reid, the outgoing Head of the Department. This event was held on the sixth floor of the Television Centre, the closest to Heaven many BBC personnel ever get. And most of the main protagonists in the 'soap' saga were there. Conversation was guarded, and polite, no-one wishing to spoil what was after all meant to be a happy occasion. But, inevitably, the talk got around to 'soaps' ... no 'soap' in particular, just 'soaps' in general. It was agreed that the most important aspect of a soap was its setting, the arena where all the drama happened. *'It doesn't matter where you put it,'* someone suggested, *'you can even set a soap in a submarine!'* But, it was what was *not* being said over the Chicken à la King that was important. Now that Elstree was a racing certainty, Julia was beginning to develop very definite ideas about where her soap should be set. Unknown to her, across the dining-table, Jonathan Powell was thinking along the same lines.

When Jonathan next asked to see Julia and Tony, they were no longer mysteriously busy. But all three were nervous. The new soap was to be a gigantic enterprise, intended on the one hand to help reverse the Corporation's controversially negative image in the press, while at the same time taking on the cut and thrust challenge of popular television, an audience the BBC had always found it hard to capture, at the time dominated by ITV. Also, the new soap would be Jonathan's first major production as Head of Series/Serials, and it had to be right!

But, there were other reasons for their nervousness, reasons closer to home. Julia and Tony did not really know Jonathan Powell. They knew his reputation, naturally. Until his recent appointment he had been a very successful producer of award-winning classic serials. How would such a BBC-2 person react to a bread-and-butter couple from BBC-1? On the surface he appeared Harrods to their Tesco's. Well, he didn't want to do the serial about mobile-homes, for a start! His reservations about the project being roughly identical to Julia and Tony's. That was the first hurdle out of the way. He thought the department should be doing something about *'London – **today***!' This effectively removed the second hurdle, as Julia and Tony had reached the same conclusion, partly as a result of the BBC considering the buying of Elstree, but mainly because they were both Londoners. Julia had gone into the meeting prepared to do battle, to insist – if she had to, that the programme be given a London setting, but Jonathan had pulled the carpet out from under her feet.

Obviously, there was no longer any reason for 'nerves'. Nervous energy was what was needed now. The energy to find the place, the people, that collection of characters who had become fed-up with just tapping on shoulders, and were now screaming into Julia and Tony's ears. 'We're over here! We're what your show should be about!' During the breathless exchange of ideas that followed, a 'Victorian Square' and 'the East-end, where that bend in the river occurs ...' were mentioned for the first time. Words like 'background', 'culture' and 'history' were thrown into the air. All very vague and haphazard, random thoughts that would probably never come to anything.

And, suddenly, that first meeting was over! Out of it had come three objectives. Firstly, the urgent need for sufficient ammunition for Jonathan to be able to shoot down the mobile-homes idea. Secondly, to commission some market-research about possible audience reaction to a programme set in the south of England. This was to satisfy 'Management', which had the idea that all successful soaps had to be located north of Luton. And finally, Julia and Tony would have to go out and create the programme. Nothing to it!

The first objective was accomplished in a weekend, touring the countryside and visiting mobile-home parks. They turned out to be eerily lifeless places, where the homes were anything but mobile. There was a marked absence of teenagers, babies, animals and meeting-places. (A notice at one such park read: NO DOGS! NO CHILDREN! Which just about summed it all up.) Added to which, the homes themselves, with their miniature rooms and vast picture windows, would be technically nightmarish to shoot! All this information was dutifully recorded for Jonathan Powell in a memo, and that was the end of that.

The second objective, the market-research, would take a little longer to achieve, until February in fact, two months away. Julia and Tony didn't give a damn about market-research (except if the results should conveniently back up their own instincts) and were determined to press on with the idea of 'London' whatever the results of the poll turned out to be.

The third objective was the hardest of all to attain, the creation of the show itself. For Julia and Tony there followed an intense period of research into the East-end of London. It involved poring over books and maps, countless field trips and coversations with real live East-enders and then, quite simply but no less exhaustively, digging into their own pasts and their own store of memories of London. Their first visit was to the Victorian Square that Jonathan had suggested. His memory of it must have been a distant one, because over the years it had become 'gentrified'. It was awash with Citroen 2CVs, stripped-pine doors with brass knockers and letterboxes and Laura Ashley curtains. (Nosey-parkers that they were, Tony and Julia peered into someone's front room, and discovered the lady of the house weaving at a loom.) The square without children or animals, quiet as the grave in fact, was vaguely reminiscent of the dreaded mobile-home park. Pushing further on into the heart of the East-end they began to get a smell of what they were looking for. They found pubs that hadn't yet become wine or cocktail bars, and still managed to retain a feeling of being local, where locals met. There were street markets that brought memories of childhood flooding back, with the litter and the noise, the bustle, the humour and the sense of people who knew each other, and who had done so for generations past.

An early 'recce pic' of a real East End location.
Attention to detail in the planning stage was vital.

Some of the market produce was not so traditional, King Edwards moving aside to allow space for okra and yams. The smells were different, too, entire stalls being given over to exotic spices. Cafés were now serving kebabs alongside the bacon sandwiches, but the English 'cuppa' hadn't yet been totally superseded. But for most people life still looked pretty hard, just as Julia and Tony thought they remembered it was like. Things had changed, that was obvious. There seemed to be fewer Jews than before, and more West Indians, Greek and Turkish Cypriots, Chinese and Asians. And what had become of all the Pie and Mash shops? There was a new sense of danger, too. More intense than in the old days. This was the sort of area where you parked your car on the outskirts and came in on foot, where you kept your hand on your purse and your wits about you, where you learned quickly not to ask uniformed policemen for directions, because you immediately became 'a marked man'. But a familiar atmosphere was still intact. There was a feeling of community and a sense of territory, a look on people's faces that seemed to be saying: *'Hurt one of us, and you hurt us all.'*

These faces which seemed to communicate so much unspoken feeling, awoke all the old sentiment which clings to today's perceptions of the East-end's past – of uncomplaining cockneys enduring the Blitz, of Arf a Mo 'Itler, of huddled bodies sheltering in the Tube as German bombs razed the two-up, two-down terraces above.

The War clings to the East-end and won't let go. More often than not the new buildings that rose in the 'sixties mark the places where bodies were pulled from rubble and whole streets that disappeared. The older members of the community remember what and who was there before the high-rise blocks and sprawling council estates, just as they remember the hardship and dangers they lived through. Maybe that shared experience brought them closer together in bonds that are still uncut?

The blue plaques that dot the East-end proclaiming that 'Marie Lloyd Lived Here', reminded the two of them that the East-end had once had a thriving music-hall tradition, too. The cockney comic was just as famous and individual as his northern counterpart, and that cockney humour lived on. Surrounded by deserted factories and shuttered shops, and faced with the ever-present threat of the dole queue, the East-enders' spirit would not go away. On one side of the street they found genuine hardship and poverty. On the other, East-end Flash, the 'business', where life was often lived off the back of a lorry, and everything seemed to drip with gold.

These were only a handful of the images, sights, sounds and smells that the devisers of the BBC's new soap brought back to the Shepherds Bush office from their explorations east of Aldgate pump. They were convinced that the location was the right one. There was such vitality, there were such possibilities for drama. Here was a community of extremes that stretched back into history. Daily, they were encountering barrow-boys just like Pete Beale, salt-of-the-earth Kathys, dotty Ethels and tough-as-old-boots Lou Beales. All the separate pieces were taking shape nicely, it was simply a question of fitting the pieces together and revealing the completed jig-saw that they both knew to be there.

Wednesday, 1 February, 1984 was the second most important day in the pre-history of EastEnders. (The most important was 2 February.) Market-research had got the results of their national poll, and asked whether Julia and Tony would like to go over to The Langham to collect them? Several questions had been put to the various panels up and down the country but the key one as far as producer and script-editor were concerned went along the lines of: 'Would you object to a new soap-opera on television from the BBC that was set in the south of England?'

People in the north of England, it seemed, welcomed the idea of a new soap set in the North, didn't mind a new soap set in the South, but wouldn't much care for a new soap set in the Midlands. People in the south of England, so the poll informed them, wouldn't object to the idea of a new soap set in the North, quite welcomed the idea of a new soap set in the South, and wouldn't much care for a new soap set in the Midlands. People in the Midlands, the report went on, welcomed the idea of a new soap on television set *anywhere*, as long as it wasn't in the Midlands! The results of the market-research only helped to reinforce what Tony and Julia had believed to be the case all along. Still, it was nice to have a bit of paper to prove it!

It was 6.15 pm and dark when they returned to Shepherds Bush, but from the car-park they could see that Jonathan Powell's office lights were still on. They decided to present him with the market-research findings, he probably had to take more notice of things like that than they did. When they reached his office on the fourth floor they found his door shut. He was in a meeting till seven. They would have to kill time for three-quarters of an hour. Jonathan's secretary, seeing the piece of paper they were carrying, said, '*I knew you wouldn't let us down.*'

She could have been speaking in a foreign language because her remark meant nothing to them. Seeing the perplexed expressions on their faces, she continued, '*The piece of paper! Jonathan wants the piece of paper!*'

It was the first they'd heard that their Head of Department needed a piece of paper. Then it dawned on them what had happened. Market-research must have tipped-off Jonathan that their results were on the way to him.

'*You mean this piece of paper?*' Julia enquired, offering the poll-results.

'*No,*' the secretary exclaimed, becoming quite shrill, '*the format! the format for the new bi-weekly! He wants it by seven o'clock tonight! He's got to sell it to Alan Hart, Controller of BBC-1, tomorrow morning! We've been trying to reach you all day!*'

Format? What Format . . .?

They fled to their office on the fifth floor, grabbed a foolscap pad and some pens, hurtled down in the lift to the ground floor and dashed across the road to Number One, Wood Lane, Albertine Wine Bar. With its clarets and quiches it was a favourite haunt of BBC types, the complete opposite of the East-end that was buzzing around in their heads, but just then it felt like neutral territory.

That was just what they needed for the awful task ahead. They ordered the largest bottle of wine in the house from Giles, the 'Guvnor', took a huge gulp, held their breath, and looked at each other across the corner table by the window. They were so shattered that they even failed to notice the sound of the London rush-hour traffic outside, only a few feet away. It was 6.20 pm, and they had to create a format, for what might prove to be one of the most important programmes in BBC-TV's history, by 7.00 pm. Forty minutes! They allowed all the sights and sounds they had taken in over the past two months to flash across their minds, and wrote down the first words that came into their heads. And, by seven o'clock, they had done it! And, what's more, typed it! At seven, on the dot, they presented themselves at Jonathan's office, and handed him a single piece of paper.

He started to read it . . .

'The bi-weekly is an on-going serial about the life of a community in the East-end of London. Being part of British history, the "East-end" location is instantly recognisable, and populated by a healthy mix of multi-racial, larger-than-life "characters". It also has an inbuilt "culture": a past... The East-end community – as personified by the "cockney" – is lively, tough, proud and sharply funny. Our group of characters is fiercely territorial: incestuous almost – and reflects how life is TODAY in a very disadvantaged part of the inner city. Our area is the poorest borough in London, with the highest crime-rate, the highest unemployment and the largest collection of deprived minority groups – yet, through all this apparent hardness, the dry, sharp and fast "cockney" wit shines through...

'The specific location is a fairly run-down Victorian Square, part council-owned, part privately-owned, and the regular characters are the inhabitants of that Square... As well as one- and two-storey houses, the Square has a pub, a mini-supermarket, a launderette, a caff, and – under the railway-bridge – the tail-end of a lively street market. 'Trendies' may soon creep into the area but for now it is basically working-class with strong "cockney" culture and values...

'Families and family-life play a large part in East-end culture: families are frequently large, matriarchal and often with several generations living under the same roof. The bi-weekly, then, is about relationships... Who's doing what, to whom, and where, will be the constant gossip of the "Square". The bi-weekly is about different types of households and different generations of people, from babies to teenagers, to adults and grandparents. It's a small community that lives a fairly closed life and has many things in common. Elements of gossip, intrigue and scandal are high on the list of everyday happenings and events...'

He read it through a second time, and nodded, 'Fine. . .' It had taken him all of sixty seconds, and he wasn't about to hand out any BAFTA Awards, or Oscars. He asked for one extra paragraph to be inserted that would strengthen the section in the format relating to the differences between all the households in the Square, and requested that the re-typed 'selling document' be in an envelope marked 'Jonathan Powell – Confidential' at Television Centre reception, by noon the next day.

A sleepless night followed, brought on, no doubt, by inevitable feelings of anti-climax. They had first been approached about the twice-weekly serial way back in March 1983. Now, a year later, all they had to show for it was 300 words on a single piece of paper. The 'format' was obviously terrible! The words and style all wrong, failing miserably to convey the vitality of the location and the liveliness of the different characters.

Jonathan clearly hated it, as would the Controller of BBC-1. Better face up to the fact, they'd blown it! Never mind, there was a possible second series of 'The District Nurse' to look forward to, and Tony had 'Cold Warrior' to complete. The great love affair with the BBC's new super-soap had turned sour. They should have stuck with mobile-home parks, or shopping arcades. Taking on the entire East-end had been a crazy dream. For the first time in months, the EastEnders waiting in the wings were silent too. Pauline, Arthur and all the others had obviously given up tapping on shoulders and had quite sensibly gone to sleep, a condition they would probably stay in for ever.

Thursday, 2 February, 1984. As requested, Tony re-typed the format. But his heart wasn't in it. He delivered it to the appointed place, and returned to his office. Julia and Jonathan attended yet another meeting of the Elstree Steering Committee. (They still had to go through the motions even if there was no end product in sight.) What was the subject under discussion this time? Unions? Transport? Money?

Julia would never be able to remember, because her thoughts were somewhere else. Walthamstow, perhaps? Or Hackney, or Bethnal Green. The standard-issue BBC-clock on the wall of the conference room crawled from 10.00 am to 12 noon. High noon! And an appointment was waiting, high up in the Television Centre.

Filled with her own sense of failure, Julia had failed to notice the nervous state that Jonathan was in. He had obviously had a sleepless night too.

She walked with him to reception where he collected the envelope. Then she escorted him, silently, to the lift area. She was almost holding his hand and treating him like a little boy. He pressed the lift button and while they waited he asked her where she was going to be for the rest of the day. Julia had intended to continue her research in the East-end that afternoon, but there did not seem much point now, so she told him she would be at her office. The lift arrived, the doors opened. Jonathan stepped in, pressed button 6. The doors closed, and Julia was on her own, with her piece of paper winging its way to the giddy heights of the sixth floor.

Julia and Tony sat in an office overlooking Shepherds Bush Green, and made small talk. Just after 12.30, Jonathan walked into the office. His demeanour had visibly altered. No longer the sweaty-palmed schoolboy, he looked like a cross between Tommy Cooper, and Biggles.

'OK, team,' he said, *'you're on!'*

It just wasn't possible! Jonathan had sold the idea to the 'sixth floor' in thirty minutes, an all-time record for the BBC. Up to then, nine weeks had been the minimum. Champagne should have been in order, but they settled for hand-shakes instead. EastEnders had officially come into existence, at last! That group of people waiting in the wings started to wake up again . . . slowly . . . opening their eyes . . . yawning. . . filling their lungs with the first draughts of the dusty air of Albert Square . . .

Soon it would be time for Angie to reach for the first gin of the day. And Pauline had to get the launderette open, and Sue the cafe. And, while Michelle got to school, Arthur had to find a job!

But the name 'EastEnders' was still a long way off. They had made a list of possible working titles. 'E8', 'Square Dance', 'Round the Square', 'Round the Houses', 'East 8', 'London Pride', were all considered and rejected. They had to have a title! They each chose one from the list and wrote them down on separate pieces of paper, and when they unfolded them found they had all chosen the same one, East 8.

Etched glass

Bathroom
Tiles

Paint Brown
+ glaze

Etched window | Q.Vic Saloon bar '84

Nuts and Bolts

Elstree Studios officially became the BBC's property when the documents were signed on 16 January, 1984. The studios were given a new name, the 'BBC Elstree Centre' and overnight East 8 had acquired a working home for itself. It had also acquired a new management to contend with, new names, new faces and a new structure to get to know, and eventually to learn to live with quite amicably. Elstree was no longer some remote prospect, it was a fact.

There was another fact staring everyone in the face. If East 8 was to hit the television screen in January 1985, then Elstree had exactly eight months to become a practical, working production centre. Unknown to all but a few, Julia and Tony had serious reservations about the programme starting its run in January. They favoured the previous November, or September even. The autumn was the best time to launch a new show as audiences were at their highest. From September through to December it was possible to consolidate a loyal audience before the viewing figures dipped again, as they always did at the beginning of every new year. But, as the true picture emerged of the massive task ahead of getting Elstree into operational order, Julia and Tony, reluctantly, had to agree to Management's original proposal. East 8 would have to wait till January to see the light of day.

January and February proved to be a very frustrating time for them. Their meetings were, sadly, few and far between. Julia still had 'The District Nurse' to finish off in Wales and Tony was heavily into the production process of 'Cold Warrior'. Julia now had the added burden of setting up Elstree, and was at the mercy, night and day, of planners, and heads of what appeared to be every BBC department in existence. Invisible demarcation lines within the internal structure of the Corporation became suddenly uncrossable, and now the unions were demanding a piece of the action. How many actors were going to be in this East 8 programme? And where would they have their tea-breaks? (Surely it would take up too much time ferrying them backwards and forwards to the canteen?) They only required one rehearsal room, didn't they? And, what on earth would they do with a recreation room? And, was it really necessary to have special rooms for dogs, and babies . . . ? And, what about staffing? How many production teams? How many people in each team? How many working hours in each week? What about factory regulations? Exactly how many

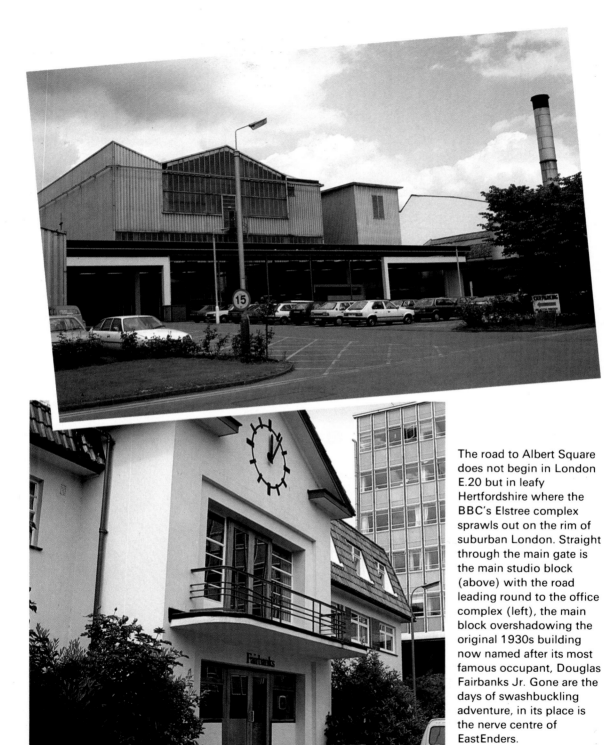

The road to Albert Square does not begin in London E.20 but in leafy Hertfordshire where the BBC's Elstree complex sprawls out on the rim of suburban London. Straight through the main gate is the main studio block (above) with the road leading round to the office complex (left), the main block overshadowing the original 1930s building now named after its most famous occupant, Douglas Fairbanks Jr. Gone are the days of swashbuckling adventure, in its place is the nerve centre of EastEnders.

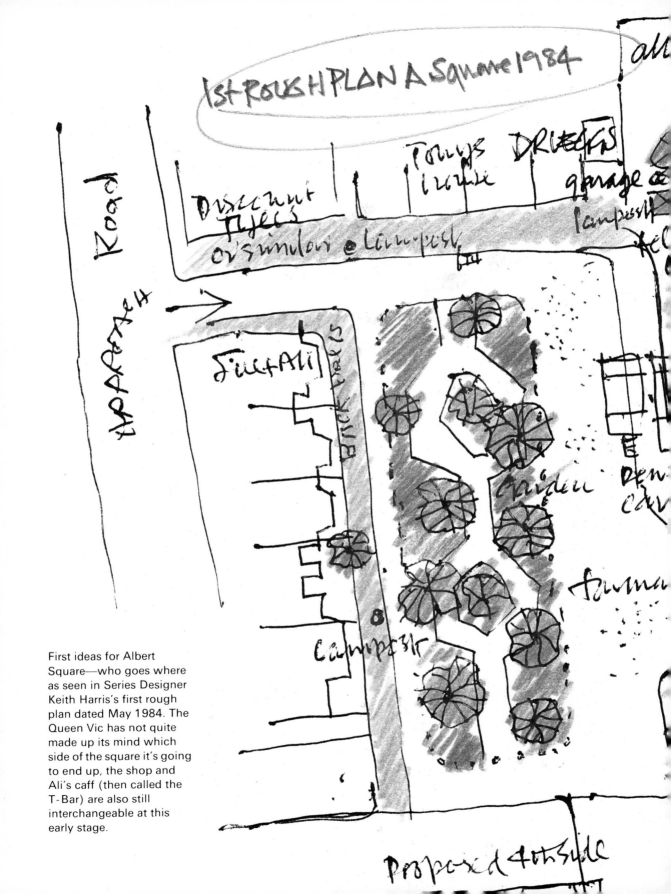

First ideas for Albert Square—who goes where as seen in Series Designer Keith Harris's first rough plan dated May 1984. The Queen Vic has not quite made up its mind which side of the square it's going to end up, the shop and Ali's caff (then called the T-Bar) are also still interchangeable at this early stage.

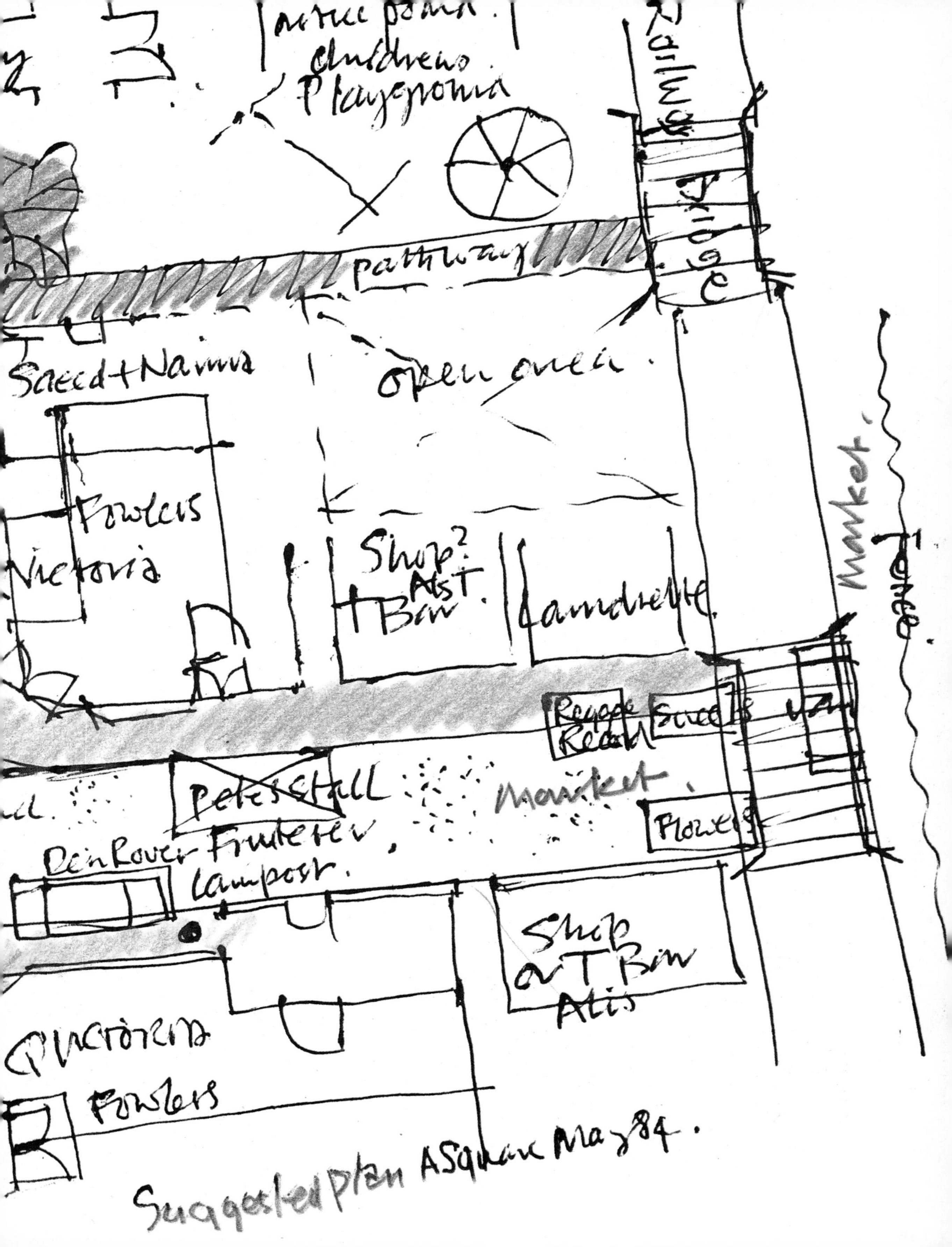

Railway Bridge

Childrens Playground

pathway

open area

Saeed + Naima

Fowlers Victoria

Shop? Ast. + Bin.

Laundrette

Market

Fence

Reggae Record

Sweets van

Flowers

Peters Stall

Den Rover Fruiterer

Compost

Market

Shop or T. Bin Atis

Victoria

Fowlers

Suggested plan A Square May 84.

'What sort of pub do we want', the creators of EastEnders asked themselves right at the beginning. The Queen Vic was going to be the heart of Albert Square, it had to be right, right enough for every viewer to feel they had been there. That meant creating a feeling that the Vic had stood for a hundred years and great attention to detail. **Above:** Keith Harris and Julia Smith check progress as the Vic rises ... but it's not opening time yet.

Left: The Vic taking shape. Great attention was paid not only to the exterior detail but the interior as this early design sketch shows (main picture). The beer pumps work, the juke box and fruit machine are all real but the whole thing had to be carefully planned to accommodate cameras, able to angle and track without making the pub look distortedly large (right).

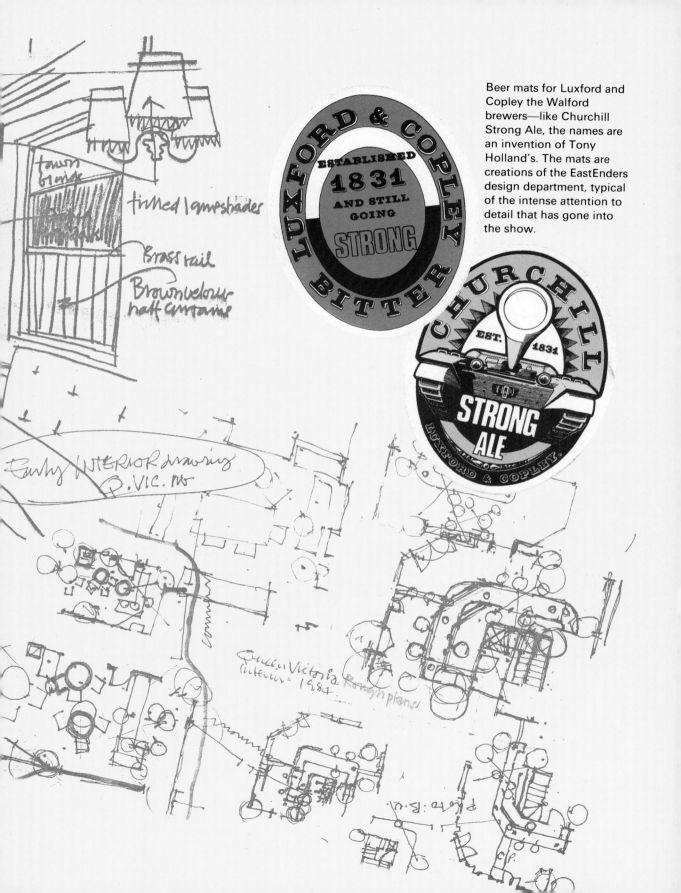

tower brick

tinted lampshades

Brass rail

Brown velour
half curtains

Early INTERIOR drawing
Q. VIC. P.H.

Queen Victoria Rough plans
Interior 1984

Plate: B.V.

Beer mats for Luxford and
Copley the Walford
brewers—like Churchill
Strong Ale, the names are
an invention of Tony
Holland's. The mats are
creations of the EastEnders
design department, typical
of the intense attention to
detail that has gone into
the show.

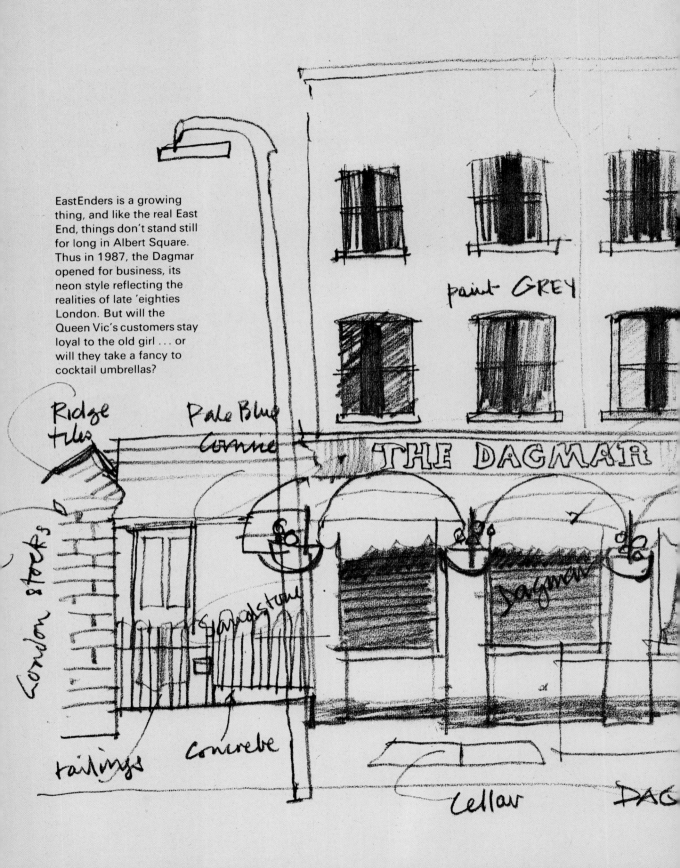

EastEnders is a growing thing, and like the real East End, things don't stand still for long in Albert Square. Thus in 1987, the Dagmar opened for business, its neon style reflecting the realities of late 'eighties London. But will the Queen Vic's customers stay loyal to the old girl ... or will they take a fancy to cocktail umbrellas?

paint GREY

Ridge tiles

Pale Blue cornice

THE DAGMAR

London stocks

Sandstone

Dagmar

railings

Concrete

Cellar

DAG

window

Brass rail

DK green felt

white sashes

Lettering gold

Shades DK green

white railing
+ rust

DK Blue

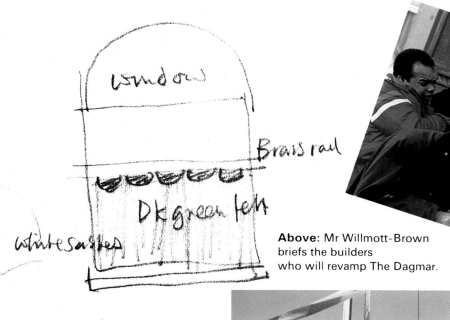

Above: Mr Willmott-Brown
briefs the builders
who will revamp The Dagmar.

Above right: The 'extension' starts
to go up on set in early 1987. The
railway bridge runs directly behind
the Dagmar (right), taking shape
according to Keith Harris's design
brief (main picture).

Above: The new set takes shape. **Right:** The betting shop and fish bar.
Below: The Green Lantern.

What area of London doesn't have a betting shop, a chippie or a Chinese takeaway? Albert Square has had all three since 1987, allowing the creators of EastEnders much greater flexibility in developing storylines and characters in new locations. **Right:** Architectural elevation for the fish bar.

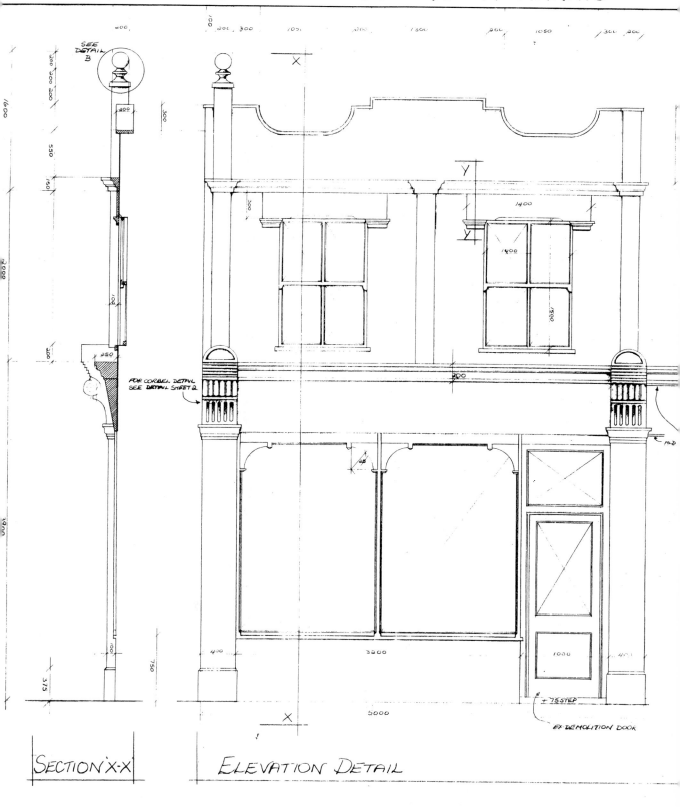

'EASTENDERS'   DES - KEITH HARRIS

SEE DETAIL B

FOR CORBEL DETAIL SEE DETAIL SHEET 2

MLD

EX-DEMOLITION DOOR

+ 75 STEP

SECTION 'X-X'

ELEVATION DETAIL

cubic feet did a human being need, by law? And how the bloody
hell is the staff going to get to these studios anyway? Elstree was
fast becoming a new Siberia. And where are the main drains?!

As these demands pressed in, Julia screamed, 'halt'! She took
a deep breath and an Anadin, and announced that, from now on,
it was going to be 'one thing at a time'. And the first thing that
had to be finalised was a working pattern. OK – it wouldn't be
right first time. It would no doubt have to be returned for revision
and re-tuning to fit realistically the special demands of Elstree.
But at least it would be one thing under everyone's belt. People
shouldn't be so tense. They had had the good fortune to enter the
game at the easy stage. For the past year, Tony and Julia had
been operating in limbo, at least the newcomers had a place to
work, and a product to work on, even if only a charmed few of
them knew the secret of what that product was.

Management reiterated what it had said from the start. East 8
was to be one of the cheapest drama productions on television,
costing not a penny more than 'Angels'. This was when Mr. Money-
Bags, Christopher d'Oyly John, Julia's logistical right-hand man,
made his second entrance, and really came into his own. Julia
used him as a sounding-board, talking off the top of her head
about possible methods of making the show, some practical, others
outlandish. He transformed these wild ramblings into sound facts;
the sort of things that planners would dismiss as arty over-indul-
gences, he translated into solid figures. One of Julia's brainwaves
was that everyone connected with the show should be housed in
one building, preferably on a single floor. Winning through this
idea and creating a single company within a sprawling bureau-
cracy, was one of the most important aspects of their start-up
period, and ultimately in the success of the show.

Few people outside of television realise how long it takes to
make programmes. Indeed, some even believe that if a programme
lasts thirty minutes on the screen, then thirty minutes is how long
it must take to produce. The truth is very different. Since the
days of 'live' telly, programme-making has become an extremely
complicated operation, full of technological wizardry that
voraciously eats into the hours in a day. Programme-making is a
slow, time-consuming business resulting in precious few minutes
'in the can' at the end to show for all the hard labour. An average
programme has rehearsals, outdoor shooting on location, interior

Left: It looks real enough
but Albert Square, Elstree,
Herts is a tribute to the
designer's and set
builders' skill. The decision
to create a permanent
exterior set rather than
shoot on location was
crucial to the show's
ultimate success.

shooting in the studio, and produces, over a period of two weeks, fifty minutes' worth of television. This breakdown doesn't include the post-production procedures of editing the sequences together and dubbing on extra sound and music. East 8 had to produce sixty minutes in a week! In other words, an extra ten minutes, in half the time!

The policy of doing 'only one thing at a time' paid off, and it seemed that a weekly working pattern was taking shape. True, bits still had to be added here and chipped away from there, but slowly things were beginning to firm up. There were to be two studio days a week, each day producing twenty-five minutes of material. And, because Julia and Tony insisted that their Square (if they ever found one!) should be seen in all weather conditions, one outside shooting-day, that produced ten minutes of material. So, the structure to make possible the recording of an hour's television every seven days seemed possible. It was a hairy schedule, certainly, but it was possible.

And now, the search for 'a Victorian Square' was on in earnest. They stole odd hours from their other shows to take time out to haunt the East-end again. Time was already running out, if East 8 was to be ready in January, then recording had to start in November at the latest. After all, there had to be time for the new studios and the new equipment to be properly tested. Also, there had to be a stockpile of episodes ready, in advance, in case of emergencies. Management wanted at least eight weeks' worth of completed programmes in hand, but Julia beat them down to three. Tony noticed that Julia was even more tired than usual, and wondered whether she would last the course. She explained that commuting to Elstree from Shepherds Bush every day was wearing her out. The minimum journey time was forty minutes, each way. That meant an extra eighty minutes added on to her working day. They realised that for other members of staff – once the system was in operation – the reverse would be the case. They would have eighty minutes taken off their working days. It would mean that on a normal studio-day an extra one hour and twenty minutes would have to be found for personnel, with a base at Television Centre, to travel to the Elstree studios and back. It shortened the whole enterprise considerably, and gave fresh grounds for alarm. Eighty minutes a day out of the system, but all those extra minutes of recording to go in! And how many more

Above: A 'recce pic' taken in the early research days.

Left: Keith Harris, the series designer whose arrival added a powerful visual dimension to the talents of the planning team. The triumvirate of producer, script editor and designer made extensive trips to the East End, filling notebooks with details of people and places. How much of the detail above, the bomb damage, the wooden shoring, the corrugated iron covered in pop posters can you see in the finished product?

vital minutes would be lost travelling to the East-end one day a week? It wasn't an easy place to get to at the best of times, what would it be like in the London rush-hour? Panic replaced alarm as it dawned on them that there were problems other than travel-time to consider. Shooting in the East-end, on a dangerously tight schedule, was not going to be a bed of roses. It's a busy, bustling, serious place where people have to get on with their lives and go about their work and where they wouldn't take kindly to a tele-vision crew moving in and calling a halt to everything.

The prospect of shooting scenes in real locations brought back a series of less than reassuring memories. 'Dr Finlay's Casebook', for example, when the lovely unspoilt Scottish village chosen as the location for the first series had to be changed by the third series, because of the sudden appearance of countless modern shopfronts. And 'Z Cars' had been the same: when gangs of local youths showered the lights and the film-crew with rocks. (And that was in the 'seventies!) What would it be like in the real East-end? Where would the technical and catering vehicles be parked? How could they bribe the residents not to repaint their houses, or change their curtains? What about insurance? The local police? And what about having to pay protection-money to the 'Firm'?

And they still had not found that Victorian Square! Fassett Square, in Hackney, was seriously considered for a while. But the huge old 'German Hospital' that dominated one side of it took it out of the running. It was the wrong 'look'. Anyway, if there was a hospital in the Square in East 8 then it would have to feature in the stories. And East 8 wasn't going to be a serial about hospitals. They had been down that road already with 'Angels'.

Keith 'Bomber' Harris, the East 8 Designer, entered, stage right, and not a moment too soon! Up to that point, the show had got a boss-lady with lots of good ideas and a script-editor with all the words. What it didn't have was the pictures. Keith would provide those pictures by dreaming up the 'look' of East 8. Like them, he had been around in the days of 'live' television, which was a promising sign. Unlike them, he had worked in the film industry, and with luck there was something from that part of his life that might be useful for East 8. Time would tell, but that was the thing they had so precious little of.

The best way to find out if the newly formed trimvirate was going to flourish was for the show's proud parents to rush Keith off to the East-end and see if it had the same effect on him as it had had on them. Would his view, through a designer's eye, match theirs? Would he have the same instinctive feelings for style, and realism? Armed with cameras and notepads, they trudged the streets of East 8, East 17, East 12, now observing and absorbing the fine detail of people and place in the whole sprawl of east London. As they walked, they talked, trying to discover what made the other tick. And, all the time, Julia and Tony were trying to 'enthuse' their new colleague with the same sense of manic energy that imbued them. On their tours, Keith started pointing things out to them, often things that they had not noticed before. A strip of corrugated iron covered in graffiti. Giant wooden supports propping up the wall of a house. A rusty railway-bridge. A line of bomb-damage running along the side of a building, on one side of it new brick, on the other old. The design of the show, Keith decided, would have to feature the ravages of the War. The place, like the people, would have a story etched into its bones. It was starting to work! The images were getting into his blood too, and all three knew that they were discussing the same dream, on the same level and in the same terms. Creative links were being formed that would help to carry them through the exhausting and frustrating months ahead.

With the arrival on the scene of Keith Harris, several problems would now disappear. But the two big problems remained, shooting in the uncontrollable setting of the real East-end, and travel-time! Julia, who had been there several times with the famous Steering Committee, decided to take Keith and Tony to visit Elstree for the first time. Perhaps it was a good idea to get away from the real East-end for a spell, and try to approach the problems sideways? The spirits of Elstree past were still there. The Art Deco buildings felt unreal, and seemed more like a film set than the future home of hundreds of working people. The long corridors were empty and echoed to the slightest sound. The trio had the distinct impression that they were trespassing, or about to embark on an eerie ghost-train ride. In the studios themselves, the old ITV cameras were still in place and they stared at the intruders like Daleks. How long was it since they had seen employment? Was Miss Piggy the last person they had photographed? The threesome shivered and went outside to get some fresh air. They also wanted to see 'the Lot'.

Hardly what they call a 'green field site', this is the patch of wasteland at Elstree seen in early 1984 from which Albert Square would rise.

A 'Lot' is a film term used to describe the large open space behind studio buildings, where often exterior sets are built. (Earlier in the day, Jonathan Powell, enquiring of Julia where she might be doing her exterior shooting, had suggested that she visit the 'Lot', as it was available for use if she wanted it.) They walked along what they took to be the perimeter road to a far corner of the site. The open ground they were passing on their left they imagined was the original car-park. To the right, behind a security fence, was the real world of Borehamwood, Hertfordshire. (Elstree studios are not in Elstree at all!) Houses, flats, shops and people. Some of them stared, as dogs barked. Was the old studio going to be opened up again, they wondered? They didn't know the half of it! The 'Lot' turned out to be a scruffy wasteland doubling as a rubbish-tip. The successful ITV comedy drama 'Auf Wiedersehen, Pet!' had been the last show recorded there, which probably accounted for the ground being completely covered in sand. It was stark and grim, and the biting wind did nothing to improve its frankly disappointing appearance. All three pulled the collars of their jackets up around their necks, and tried to imagine what the 'Lot' must have been like in the good old days.

Perhaps they were all thinking what Julia was thinking – why shouldn't it come back to life again, as a run-down Victorian square, in the London of 1985? They'd cracked it! They would build their *own* East-end in the middle of Hertfordshire! The two big problems would be removed in a single swipe. They would have their own controllable patch and there would be no travel worries. In the distance, they could see a concrete and glass tower-block, if Keith was to build the Square in a certain way, it would be possible to see that tower-block, and give the location more of an inner-city feel. That tower-block could actually become part of the programme's dreaded off-stage monster, the 'Estate'. It was a deliciously fortuitous entry of reality into the illusion they were convinced they could create.

Houses could go here. A central threadbare garden could go there. A pub on that corner. The start of a market next to the pub, and a railway-bridge, with a small street connecting them. And one family could live in this house, another in that one ... The chat suddenly stopped. Was anyone actually breathing? Without realising at the time what she was doing, Julia had picked up a stick from a pile of junk to one side, and had been drawing

Scrawled in the sand left behind by *Auf Wiedersehen Pet* on the empty lot at Elstree, the first sketch of Albert Square scratched by Julia Smith.

diagrams in the sand. The three of them looked down at the results of her handiwork ... She added a final flourish to her efforts and they all stood back to get a better view. Cameras were produced and the drawing in the sand was recorded for posterity. Julia had sketched what was eventually to become Albert Square, Walford, E20. Underneath she had written 'East 8'.

Now they would need Christopher D'Oyly John, the production associate, to produce statistics to convince Keith Anderson (heading the Elstree Steering Committee, representing Planning and Finance) that in the long run it would be cheaper to build a square.

'How long a run?'

'Well ... say three years.'

'Prove it!'

And Mr Money-Bags set out to do just that, helped by some, hindered by others, like design group, for instance, Keith Harris' bosses.

'It isn't possible to build a Victorian Square in only seven months. It will fall down!'

Keith wanted the set completed at least two months before shooting started, so that it would have plenty of time to 'weather'.

'Will you need planning permission?'

'What do you mean, you want the set to have a life-expectancy of ten years?!'

'What happens when the show's a flop?'

'Anyway, it will look terrible! You can only achieve real art in a real location. Everybody knows that.'

Somehow Mr Money-Bags produced the statistics that convinced the planners, and the go-ahead was given for the Square to be built on the 'Lot' at Elstree. Despite Design Group ... *'Up yours, darlin'.'*

Keith chose two very clever young design-assistants to complete the design-team, Gina and Peter, and Gina's first task was to produce the very first model of the Square. When Keith wasn't tramping all over the East-end with Julia and Tony seeking out and photographing houses, pubs, cafes, markets and launderettes that were to be the prototypes for the set, he was at auctions buying up old doors, windows and frames. Or, he was finding out where the largest trees could be bought, or paving stones, and, bricks. And was it cheaper to make the market stalls, or buy them? Keith remembered how things were done in the old days, and the old forgotten techniques. He surrounded himself with a group of talented and highly-skilled craftsmen from the BBC who began the awesome task of constructing roofs, walls, tiles, plasterwork bricks, chimneys and ornate metal railings to surround the central garden area of the Square. At the same time an outside firm was brought in to augment their work and dig the foundations, erect the skeletal framework that the set would eventually be built on to, build the roads and construct the low brick walls. They also had to sink the drains for the Square, praying all the time that they would not encounter the main Elstree sewer which was rumoured to cross underneath the 'Lot'.

All this activity just for the exterior set. The interior, studio sets would have to wait for a while, as 'Bomber' Harris and his private army had quite enough to be going on with.

Julia had many pet hates and working in London was one of them. She had avoided it for years, preferring the atmosphere and working conditions of the regions. 'Angels' had been recorded in Birmingham, and 'The District Nurse' in Cardiff. There was one important difference between London and the regions about the way you made your programmes. In the regions you used the same cameramen, lighting and sound supervisors – in rotation – out on location and in the studio. In London, you did not. The studio operation was handled by Television Centre, the film operation from Ealing and the Outside Broadcast unit by Kendal Avenue, each with their own personnel who could not be interchanged. The good thing about the regional system was that it produced programmes with a unified style, as well as a group of satisfied programme-makers who were not artificially split up into different territorial areas. The bad thing about the London system was that you could end up with one show being made by three different groups of people. Julia wanted the regional system for East 8. If it was good enough for Birmingham and Cardiff, why not London? Basically all she wanted was two cameras, and some recording equipment that could be stored in a small van. Didn't the BBC in London need to be more progressive in its thinking anyway?

And so a brand new unit was to be invented, to be known as The Insert Unit. But John Lightfoot, who was put in charge of the unit's development, was presented with a set of prior conditions. First and foremost, it must be simple, just two cameras and a simple cutting-device to get from one picture to another. Too complicated and it would impinge on the territory of the Outside Broadcast unit, and threaten their status. There wasn't even to be a seat in the van for the director, he would have to be content to work outside, with the actors, with only a tiny monitor to observe the progress of the recording. No heavy film equipment was to be used either, as that would impinge on the territory of the Film Department, and threaten their status. If successful, the unit was to be a cross between film and television techniques. And, if the unions agreed, London studio-personnel would be able to work outside as well as inside, for the very first time. The final test of the unit would come when it could be taken outside the confines of Elstree and be allowed to operate in a real location. But there would be a three-year wait before that was to happen. Without getting the logistics right there could be no show but meanwhile the characters in their heads were still relentlessly slouching towards Albert Square to be born. They were beginning to get impatient.

'What about me?' asked Pauline Fowler. *'Am I going to be pregnant in episode one, or what? And will I be allowed to smoke?'* *'Sorry,'* said Julia, *'bit busy at the moment, Pauline, speak to you later . . .'*

Reg Cox, worse for wear from lunchtime boozing, slumped into his frayed armchair: *'D'you mean I won't have a single line of dialogue? Not even one?'* *'Tied up at the moment, Reg,'* Tony replied, *'will try and fit you in next week ...'* And, Nick Cotton ... Who? Who the hell's Nick Cotton?!

The telephone lines between Shepherds Bush and Elstree were getting jammed, and Tony and Julia were lucky if they managed to cram into their days even thirty seconds of conversation with each other.

'British Actors' Equity would like a meeting with Julia to discuss what form the actors' contract might take for the bi-weekly ...'

'Can Tony and the BBC's copyright blokes attend a meeting with the Writers' Guild to sort out a possible writers' deal for this East 8 programme ...?'

'Julia, British Telecom's here. They want to know how many phone-lines we're going to need. Oh, and that man's still waiting downstairs for your answer about what colour the offices are going to be ...'

'Tony? At last! You've been engaged for ages! Look, I represent several exciting new writers. I think you should meet them about your "Estate" thing ... Oh ... "East 8" ... ah ... Well – I've got a couple of writers who were actually born in the East-end. Any good to you? ...'

'Julia? At last! I don't know why your secretary keeps fobbing me off ... Look, darling, about casting. I represent some lovely people. If you could send me a breakdown of all the characters, I'll make a list of suggestions for you. Where exactly is this Estate going to be set? Oh ... "East 8" ... Ah ... Well – I've got a couple of actors who **live** *in the East-end. When can you see them?'*

Ring-ring!

'Tony? It's Julia. We must meet ...'

'Julia? It's Tony. How the hell am I supposed to give Keith a list of permanent studio sets when all we've got is one bit of paper ...?'

'Tony? It's Julia. How much money do you think I should allow for cars?'

'Julia? It's Tony. I've worked it out. We need scrips by June.'

'Are you mad? 'Costume' wants scripts in **May!** *They've got a deadline to meet.'*

'Deadline! Don't talk to me about deadlines! ''Costume can wait!'' '

'Tony? It's Julia. Can we meet . . . ?'

'Sorry, love. Just been told that we can't film ''Cold Warrior'' at Heathrow Airport. And Michael Denison's in a tizz about some dialogue he wants rewritten. Speak to you soon . . .'

The frustrations were mounting. Mr Money-Bags was being attacked from all directions for information. But information about what? East 8 was just a bare carcass of bones. Without the flesh, how could he possibly give out information?

'Julia? It's Tony. Can we meet . . . ?'

'Sorry, mate. Got to dash off to a meeting with the technicians . . .'

The tensions were already becoming unbearable when it was discovered that the studio's wiring was positively *dangerous*. Everything would have to be re-equipped, including a new control room, a new lighting gallery, and a new viewing-room for Julia and Tony that had to be private. More questions were queuing up for an answer, how many cameras in the studio? Four conventional and one hand-held . . . one can be used as a standby but there must be four operational at all times! Editing . . . My God – editing . . . How much? As little as possible. How many days? Two – can't spare any more time. When? Have to be weekends to fit in with the schedule. (Weekends?! Peak time for the editing department. What about Grandstand? OK – make it a day and half then. Saturday morning. And all day Sunday.) What about a second edit? Second edit?! What do you think this is? 'Bleak House', or something?

'Bleak House' it was not. It was a bread-and-butter programme that probably wouldn't win any posh awards, but might capture a decent-sized audience. And facing that fact sorted out a lot of things. Who wanted a large audience, anyway? Why should the Corporation enter the free for all of down-market drama? A lot of people in television, probably those who only make their shows for other programme-makers, could not understand why the BBC should want to popularise itself. 'Drama' should be an elitist pursuit, with productions aimed at chasing after awards, not mere audience-figures.

Keith Harris got a bellyful of it from Design Group, and Julia and Tony picked up the negative feelings from other producers, script-editors and organising staff. Entire departments were being split down the middle, those in favour of the soap, those against. It became the talk of the wine-bar crowd. Who in their right mind would want to slog all the way to Elstree (by now known as 'Hellstree') to work on a soap? . . . scraping the barrel a bit, isn't it? How low can you get . . . ? Julia and Tony bit their lips and kept their chins up, in an effort not to let on to anyone how bitterly hurt they were by all this. It seemed their only crime was loving the audience. And if you weren't in television to reach an audience, then why were you in it?

Out of all this conflict, the Elstree spirit was born. Friends loyal to Julia and Tony started to rally round, people stopped feeling hard done by as they realised they were all in this together and that East 8 could be made to work.

Throughout this period, Jonathan Powell and the top management at Television Centre stood behind them. Right then the Sixth Floor had worries of its own. For a variety of reasons the BBC was in the political doghouse and relations with the government were deteriorating. The Peacock Committee, looking into the way the BBC was run and funded, was looming. It was deemed essential that the BBC could show it still had a feeling for what its customers, the licence-fee payers, actually wanted. It needed a popular success, and not just a success – it had to be a *monster* success! But Julia and Tony were shielded from all this. It was never made totally clear to them the weighty burden that they would have to carry on their shoulders. If it had been, it would probably have destroyed them, and the new baby would have been still-born.

'Tony? It's Julia. We must meet ... The phones never stop ringing. What does it matter what colour the office-walls are? What's the point of a schedule if there aren't any characters, stories and scripts? Let's get the hell away from here ...'

They went to see their trusty travel agent. 'Rose,' Julia began, 'Find us somewhere where there's a little sun, a lot of peace and quiet and no phones ... by the end of the week.'

Lanzarote is the northern-most island in the Canaries, pinpoints of volcanic rock rising out of the Atlantic off the west coast of Africa. Some of the beaches have black sand, which is sometimes disconcerting for sun-bathers who might be forgiven for thinking they were stretched out on a coal face. Not that there are many sun-worshippers in Lanzarote in March, as it can get very chilly. Lanzarote is an ideal place for a holiday. The light is very beautiful, particularly at dusk, the booze is cheap, all in all, the perfect place to laze about in, swim or windsurf and change from English pale to golden brown. But, when Julia Smith and Tony Holland got off their plane at Arrecife airport on Thursday 8 March, 1984, any thought of being on a holiday was the last thing on their minds.

They were there to *work*, probably harder than they'd ever done before in their whole lives. The hand-baggage consisted of a portable typewriter and a case stacked with A4 paper. Their 'office' was situated at the San Antonio apartments, Playa los Pocillos, midway between the airport and the popular tourist resort of Puerto del Carmen. They had until 22 March, fourteen days (twelve if you discounted the two travelling days) to create twenty-three characters, a skeletal overall storyline for the first three years and the first twenty storylines in detail. The weather during those two weeks was as black as the sand with a howling wind that rattled the sliding-doors that opened on to their balcony. Bad weather was a good sign, it meant one less reason to want to go out, one less distraction when they could hardly afford any.

Before even removing the protective case from the typewriter they established what their daily routine was going to be. What time they would rise in the morning. How long they would work, before breaking off for a snack lunch. When they would stop working in the evening. Whether they should cater for themselves at night, or dine out. Should they allow themselves days off? If the sun came out, could they treat themselves and cram in the odd hour or two of sun-bathing, so that they might return to England at least pink?

The 'creative process' is impossible to define. Some prefer to conduct the tricky business alone. Others would rather share the agony with a partner, someone they can bounce their ideas off. Tony and Julia favoured the latter approach. A creative partnership demands enormous trust between the parties involved. It's strenuous and lively but needs humour and the ability to forgive and forget. It's about taking risks and not worrying about looking foolish if things go wrong. Those whose business it is to invent dramatic characters often learn as much about themselves as they do about the 'people' they are creating.

By now they had established the place, the East-end of London. And they had focused on a specific part of that place, a run-down Victorian square. And they had even managed to fill that specific part of the place with some bricks and mortar, houses, a tower-block, a pub, a cafe, a shop, a launderette and a market. But who lived there? And what sort of people were they? And when the audience first meets them in January, 1985, what has happened in their lives up till then?

Tony and Julia started talking . . .

Right from the start they had wanted the backbone of the programme to be a family. A large family, in the old East-end tradition. The sort of family that's on the way out even in the East-end, as people emigrate to Eastbourne, or trek east to that English county that every day gets more and more like the East-end except with a pony in the paddock and a Jag on the gravel drive, Essex, Ilford, Romford, Chelmsford . . . and all points east to Southend, Westcliff, Shoeburyness and Leigh-on-Sea. But families like that did still exist in the East-end, those that had refused to pull up their roots and leave the home that had probably been passed on, mother to daughter, mother to daughter, for generations. Julia and Tony were helped here by Tony Holland's own background. His mother originally came from one of those East-end families, the Thirkettles, from Walthamstow. There were four sisters, Lou, Doris, Sis and Ethel. Tony's mum was the youngest.

Lou married Albert and became a Beale. Doris and Sis married two brothers, Bert and Bill, and became Mears. And Ethel had married John and become a Holland. Since childhood Tony had ducked in and out of the life of this large family. A family getting larger every year, as the next generation appeared. Tony's cousins, Peter and Pauline Beale, Shirley and Graham Mears. Ken Mears. And Tony's brothers, Allan and Bryn.

By sweeping aside a lot of cobwebs from his brain, Tony recalled the events in that family's history – Christmas, weddings, funerals. If he tried really hard he could even remember snatches of conversations. Fights. (His nickname had been 'Bruiser'!) Christmas presents. The tea-time menu ... It was obvious that Tony would have to undertake the job of creating what was eventually to become the Beales and the Fowlers, eight of those elusive twenty-three characters. It would not be accomplished overnight and would remove him from the working partnership probably for several days. So what would Julia do in the meantime? They decided to postpone the birth of the 'family' till they had some other people to work on, and they talked some more.

Sometimes these chats would go on for hours and seem to have no apparent sense of direction, free-wheeling exchanges that produced maybe only a single idea. But that single idea could lead on to another and on to another, and maybe a 'character' would be the end result. Julia had been very taken with a woman they had seen in a pub in Hackney. She had been elderly, probably a widow, and had bright ginger hair crowning a face made-up to rival a neon sign. She laughed a lot, was obviously the life and soul of the party, and had a little dog, with a red ribbon on its head, tied in a bow. A single, older woman. Surely there was a place for such a person in the 'Square'? And if there was to be a single older woman, why not a single younger woman, with a baby perhaps? ... And a single man, too. A doctor, maybe? Jewish ...?

The work-pattern was dividing up neatly. Tony would tackle the families, those that were related, while Julia kicked-off with the single people. The talking stopped, and the work began. Frantic scribblings, crossings out and sharpening of pencils. Like the Hollywood cliché of the struggling author, the sitting-room floor was soon covered with screwed-up balls of paper. During this part of the process, work in progress was seldom, if ever, discussed, even over dinner. Partly because at the end of each day their brains were quite simply exhausted and all they wanted to talk about was light inconsequential things ... like the fact that the wind was getting up again, and now it was even starting to rain. But also because they were afraid to reveal what was happening right in front of them. They were afraid that if they showed their hands too soon, the bubbles would burst. At night, behind the closed doors of their rooms, sleep was hard to come by. That group of characters waiting so patiently, no longer needing to scream to be let out, was still persistent enough. They knew they were slowly getting some flesh on their bones, and were only concerned to make little suggestions now and then ...

'LOUISE (Lou) BEALE. A lively 70 year old. Archetypal East-end mother-earth figure. Fat, funny, sometimes loud, often openly sentimental. An obsessive view of family ... she can be a stubborn, cruel "old-bag" when she wants to be, sometimes keeping "atmospheres" going for months. It was always Lou's house that was used for the big family celebrations. Especially Christmas. Twenty or more people crammed into a tiny house. Five sisters wedged into a miniscule kitchen; drinking gin and orange; wearing funny hats; all wearing aprons; laughing raucously and trying to cook a huge dinner at the same time. Lou's was also the meeting place for the family Sunday teas. Ham, or tinned salmon salad. Bread and butter. Jelly and tinned cream. And, tea ... The changing face of the area (especially the immigrants) is a constant source of fear to her. But then she doesn't go out much. She prefers to be at home, or on a trip down memory-lane: day trips to Southend – the Kursal, Rossi's ice-cream and a plate of cockles; one wonderful week's holiday in a caravan in Clacton; fruit picking in Essex; Christmas; weddings; street parties ... She has a soft spot for her son, Pete ...'

At this stage in her creation, Lou didn't realise that she had a friend in the Square who went back almost as far as she did. Julia hadn't quite finished putting her down on paper ...

'ETHEL (May) SKINNER. Most of her money goes on food for her dog, Willy, a Yorkie, and booze for herself. She has a hopeless memory for actual facts but can tell endless stories about pre-war London, her childhood, and, above all, the war. She does miss the friendliness of the old East-end ... She has false teeth and red hair: those are the two things you most notice about her – then, the dog ... Her greatest joy is telling fortunes, cards, teacups and palm-reading. "I've got the gift," she says ... Born 1920, in Camden Town ... left home, aged 16, to work for a posh Hackney family, as a general undermaid ... Ethel came home one day to find her street destroyed by a doodlebug. Her parents had been in the house ... Ethel met William, a docker, and they married when Ethel was 25 ... Ethel and William had no children ... As a youngster, Ethel would have been a page three girl, a real pin-up ...'

Little did Ethel know that she would end up living on the first floor of a house owned by the local doctor. How could she? He hadn't been invented yet! One thing at a time, remember? Julia started on him the next morning . . .

'DR HAROLD LEGG. (His parents took the name Legg from the street they used to live in) . . . the tough time came in the mid-'thirties when the extreme right and Mosley on one hand, and the persecution of Jews in Europe on the other, forced him as a bright teenager to become positively aware of racism, freedom and persecution. He didn't become a communist, he didn't start hating all Germans – but he did stop going to the Synagogue . . . he decided as he approached seventeen to become a doctor . . . perhaps he should have been a musician? Like his Uncle Leon . . . He saw the air-raid casualties . . . it reinforced his passion for the underdog . . . he met and fell in love with a young (non-Jewish) nurse – they were married when he was twenty-one . . . she was in the garden when a dog-fight took place overhead, and the German pilot dropped his bomb in order to get away. The corner of the square went – so did she.'

So, that was where the bomb fell. They didn't know that before. Better have some modern-type houses beside the pub. (Phone Keith?) Why wasn't the pub itself affected? Better foundations, perhaps, because of the cellars? Better check that out when they get back to England . . .

At the end of each day, they would read what the other had written, make suggestions and changes, and then Tony would 'turn them into prose' and type them up . . . Ethel and Lou would have to be altered because they now knew each other. Ethel would have to be changed anyway, because she's living in the doctor's house. Who else lives in the doctor's house . . .? And, the next day, they'd start all over again!

'PAULINE. Pete's twin sister. Forty, and a chip off the Louise block. Plucky, and determined to battle through whatever the odds. A warm, practical, unsophisticated woman: you stand by your man, do your duty, fight for your kids and have a roast for Sunday dinner . . . She's also pregnant . . . She actually remembers her dad saying: *"Two things we don't discuss in this house are*

religion and politics.'' She also remembers her dad smoked a pipe, and wishes her husband did too. She loved her dad very much . . . Maybe she didn't go into the marriage with quite the right spirit? She was due to be chief bridesmaid at her sister's wedding but she'd got the flu and was confined to bed. Arthur, someone she'd known from school, was given permission to visit the invalid upstairs. He found himself proposing to her. Years later he said: *''It was to cheer her up really.''* And Pauline found herself accepting too . . . she's very fond of her twin brother, Pete. (And knows that he's mum's favourite.) She's very conventional, and the salt of the earth. Jolly. Rounded. Someone you can get your arms round. She doesn't trust skinny people . . .'

'**ARTHUR.** Rock-solid and reliable. Has an instinctive (unintellectual) wisdom . . . He cries openly at funerals, loves his wife, is strict with his children, doesn't drink a lot, supports Arsenal, votes Labour and would never walk down the street carrying flowers. He worked in a factory – but was made redundant, and has been unemployed for a year . . .'

'MARK AND MICHELLE. Mark will be leaving school at Easter and is fairly certain to be joining his dad in the dole queue. Michelle has another year of schooling ... Mark is a very tough little lad, and at a very dodgy stage in his development ... There's a kind of amoral streak in his nature ... The area does have a brutalising effect on a lot of its youngsters. ... Michelle is obviously more on the straight and narrow. ... Unlike her brother, she gets what "things" she wants, by doing part-time work. "Saturday girl" at the local hairdressers, and two late shifts a week at a hamburger place. She's into Reggae ...'

'PETER (Pete) BEALE. Runs a fruit and veg stall in the market ... married very young to Pat – it turned out to be a total disaster. They were too young, rushing into a difficult life for all the wrong reasons, and truthfully, his wife was a vicious shrew ... he divorced his wife and married Kathy when he was 24 ... Ian was born a year later. It took Kathy and Pete about 10 years to woo Lou round to the idea of their marriage, and she can still sometimes be a bit cutting about it ... She doesn't believe in divorce. ... He did have crazy dreams of making something of himself, he was going to be a singer, a red-coat, run his own hotel ... On special occasions it's always Pete who's the life and soul of the party ... His two sons by his first marriage are nineteen and twenty and he hardly sees them. ... If it wasn't for Thatcher, he'd consider voting Tory ... Never works on the anniversary of his dad's death, and with Pauline, escorts his mum to the cemetery. He has a good relationship with Kathy, emotionally and sexually. (Maybe he's a little concerned that she's keeping her good looks a bit longer than he is ... ?) ...'

'KATHY BEALE. A hard childhood. An overcrowded, strict one – with no money but bags of misery. You either give in to that, or you rebel ... A lot of people think she's hard. The exterior is certainly tough – it's had to be. From a childhood surrounded by too many brothers, a heavy drinking father, and a submissive mother. A knowledge that you came from the "slum end" of the borough. The tattiest school uniform. The least money. To be the poorest of the poor was a hell of a thing to fight against ... by patience, persistence, cool dignity, the refusal to argue and fight back like a fishwife, wooing, cajoling and setting a good example,

she and Pete finally became accepted – even by Lou ... a moral woman with a firm sense of right and wrong, and good and bad. She finds it almost impossible to tell a lie, bitch – or accept the goods Pete sometimes brings home that have fallen off the back of lorries. It's as if she's had such a long hard fight to be thought of and accepted as a respectable/decent person, that she's frightened of anything happening that might soil that image. A great sense of humour ... she's ''practical'' in that she doesn't shatter Pete's dreams even though she knows none of them will ever materialise, because she realises to do so would also shatter him ... Kathy *never* forgets a favour ...'

'**IAN BEALE.** There is a pressure from home to do well at school and he may be a bit worried that he's not doing as well as they hope. The shadow of his father (however fictional the image is) and the pressure to be a man's man and a chip off the old block might cause trouble in the future. A point is going to be reached when Ian is going to have to assert himself as himself. He can't allow his father to live his life, by proxy, through him. Or, maybe he can ...?'

The Beales and The Fowlers, still very rough round the edges, were complete. It just needed Julia to finish off that single young woman ...

'**MARY SMITH.** Aged nineteen. Mary was brought up in Stockport. Her parents were Irish Catholics ... Her father is a long-distance lorry driver ... When she left school Mary could hardly read or write, she didn't learn because she didn't want to ... She gave no trouble, no aggro, but no-one took any notice of her ... Her mother nagged her about her soul ... At fifteen she went to a gig with a crowd of people from school and in one night her life changed. ... In one night, she fell in love with a band, a man and a culture. She had found her own religion. ... She became pregnant ... Semi-literate, unskilled and at the same time ashamed ... She couldn't go back to the oppressive society of her childhood, where everybody judged everybody and where she would be labelled, even by her mother, as a ''loose woman'' ... She wouldn't have an abortion ... She drifted into our area, and became one of the single parent families that congregate there ... Will she be a survivor, or a loser? . . . Over the months she may develop a fear of authority . . . maybe she will be forced to drift into a life of prostitution . . .'

Eleven down, that left twelve to go. The invention of the regular cast of a continuous serial, must take into account certain considerations. There has to be a varied group of characters, so that several different sections of the audience have someone to identify with. The larger the mix of people the easier it will be to find stories that have variety, interest and mileage. And, if the programme is to be even half-way realistic, it must also reflect the cross-section of society that actually exists in the real location. What was wanted for East 8 then, was different sexes, ages, classes, religions and races. The ethnic minority groups had been the hardest to research. No matter how far you dug inside yourself, it just wasn't possible to produce a Turkish Cypriot from your past. True, there were lots of useful books to turn to. But books didn't always give the complete picture. Also, there were official agencies one could approach. But, in their experience, official agencies were inclined to adopt an official line, wanting things played by the book and not as they really were. Fortunately for Julia and Tony, they had been in the forefront of the move towards 'integrated casting' in television and so had already come up against many people of different ethnic origins. Over the years a lot of these people had become friends. And, being genuinely interested in people, but also incurably inquisitive, they had both pumped these friends for information about their origins and lifestyles. It was all to help in the creation of East 8's most recent immigrants.

'SAEED AND NAJMA JEFFERY. He is a quarter English, three-quarters Bengali and she is wholly Bengali. Their parents were originally from Bangladesh, formerly East Pakistan, and they are Muslims and cousins . . . He left school at eighteen and went to cramming college for a year . . . In despair, his parents sent him back to India. He had always felt an outsider in England because he's an Indian (the "paki" at school) but he didn't fit in in India either. The other Bengali children of his generation called him "Sahib" . . . Najma had an easier childhood . . . She became aware that she couldn't accept the traditional role of an Indian wife, but she wasn't enough of a rebel to leave home and adopt a totally different lifestyle ... Saeed's mother's father became seriously ill. It was decided that Saeed's parents, rather that Najma's, should return home to India, and a hasty marriage was arranged between Najma and Saeed so that the young couple could then run the food store ... They are in a confusing situation, accepting the customs of their parents, yet – because of having been born, brought up and educated in this country – feeling that they're slightly English ... Neither of them is particularly docile, having lived through the jungle of the school playground, and the cut and thrust of working-class urban life ... Saeed and Najma will make a big effort to mix, and most of the time, fail ... Saeed might even visit the pub, and try to give the impression that he's a real cockney ... but he wouldn't want to go home to a cockney wife ...'

'ALAN AND KEVIN CARPENTER. Alan is Caribbean: one of the "came here when ten" from an idyllic life in Trinidad with his gran ... A confusing childhood and, at first, he hated England. He felt different, felt coloured, suffered abuse from the white kids ... He met Hannah. She was several cuts above him socially. He liked the idea of a "princess" and she liked the idea of "a bit of rough". In the beginning this made their marriage all the more exciting ... But he was short on staying power ... In and out of jobs ... Boredom always setting in early ... A constant desire for "change" at any price ... Hannah meanwhile became more and more stubborn ... They set themselves on a collision course ... Hannah became too housebound, houseproud, too disciplined with the two children, too rigid, not seeing the wood for the trees. Alan became too anarchic, too sleeping-around, too devil-may-care and up-yours, frequently not seeing the wood for the booze ... Perhaps if they split, they could find themselves again ...? Alan has bought a house in the Square. His sixteen-year-old son Kevin wants to stay with his dad ... How would Alan react to the discovery that Kevin's visiting his mother? How would Kevin react to his father trying to "smuggle in" a woman for the night? And, how would dad react to son doing the same thing? What happens when they're competing for the same woman? As he wants to leave his mark – physically – on the walls of the building, so he wants to leave his mark on his son. Will Kevin take it, or leave it ... The house is the framework. The container ... It will change its personality as the owners find theirs ...'

'CHRIS AND SUE OSMAN. Chris is a Turkish Cypriot, his wife, Sue, is English, and they run the cafe just off the Square. In the evenings, Chris is also a minicab driver. They have a nine-month-old son named after Chris' dad – Hassan – and they are devoted to him ... Chris was born in Cyprus in 1957. But, as it turned out in 1974, he was a Turk in a Greek zone. A refugee-camp followed. Then, the family was resettled in a Turkish zone. But, it never felt like home, and there was no money so, in 1975, they came to London ... Chris married Sue in 1982 ... Chris is basically lazy, and a gambler. Not (yet) a compulsive gambler – but he is a passionate one ... He's a bit of a peacock. He expects to be waited on hand and foot ... Chris is always having to prove himself ... Sue was the child of older parents. Affection was what was missing from the house. No real love, no fire and no closeness. She never saw her parents touch each other, or demonstrate tenderness ... Is Sue actually looking for a bad time in life? Is she the big martyr? Perhaps convinced that her parents had no affection for her, she can't understand anyone else doing so. She's a very insecure woman – furiously jealous and possessive, and always accusing Chris of being unfaithful. She's always putting herself in the position of being the victim. Sometimes she nearly goads Chris into hitting her, and perhaps one day she'll succeed ... A gigantic, self-imposed, chip on her shoulder ... she needs dramas – it's something she's good at. She is a poisonous bitch, but it's important that we understand why ...'

There were only a few more days left of the 'holiday' and six more people to conjure up out of thin air, and there were still lots of work to do on all those already created. For instance, the names Saeed and Najma were the same as two Bengali friends of Tony's. He'd been fortunate enough to be invited to the wedding part of their arranged marriage. It was decided to change Najma to 'Naima', to protect the innocent! They had also made a mistake, of course, giving Chris Osman, a Muslim, a 'Christian' name. Chris later became Ali! Which meant that they now had two characters whose names began 'AL ...' So, Alan became 'Tony'. And, for reasons long since forgotten, Kevin became 'Kelvin'. They seemed to be putting off creating the occupants of the pub. Was it because, even then, they had an intuition that that particular household was going to provide so much action? What else was missing?

They both felt that to help complete the community there was a need for a male character in his early twenties. He had to be someone a bit different. Not brash and confident like a lot of the older men. And, not as boisterous as the younger ones. A bit of a loner perhaps, maybe someone forced to be a loner. A square peg in a round hole? A person who stuck out like a sore thumb? Someone who was at his happiest in a 'group' but constantly found that he couldn't fit into one – or couldn't find one, even. There was the memory of conversations Julia and Tony had had in the past about his life in the army. (He came from an army family. Father and both brothers being in uniform, too.) Surely the all-male camaraderie of the barrack-room, the fact that life was structured for you, and even the security of a uniform that made you all look alike, was the 'group' setting of all time? Suppose our young man had been a soldier? And, what's more, supposing he had been a very happy one. What sort of person would he have turned into if he'd been forced to quit the army? Say, on medical grounds, or something like that. And so, Lofty was born . . .

'LOFTY (George) HOLLOWAY. Born of a working-class London family, which was very respectable: C of E and ex-army . . . Lofty grew up in a house where his father was only really happy when reminiscing about his army days and his mother was ultra-possessive and narrow minded . . . His friends were always vetted . . . He grew up to despise his mother and have a tolerant pity for his father . . . His best moments came in the Boy Scouts, the summer camp, and the feeling of belonging . . . On his eighteenth birthday, he walked into an Army Careers Office and from then till the age of twenty-one had the happiest years of his life in the RASC. . . . He adored the army – it gave him a uniform, and set the limits . . . Then the shock – he was discovered to be physically unfit . . . Dormant asthma . . . He was invalided out of the service . . . And, he had no taste for civilian life . . . His Auntie Irene (now in a hospice) secured the flat above Ethel's for Lofty . . . He misses the security of the Army . . . He works at the pub – cash in hand . . .'

One more hole had been plugged and finally someone was occupying that vacant flat in Doctor Legg's house. But still there remained a gap, and not just the elusive pub, something to do with 'different classes ... trendies, and gentrification'. They suddenly remembered that woman they'd seen in her living-room in the real up-market square, weaving at a loom. No, she wasn't quite right, their square hadn't gone that far yet. But, it was moving that way, slowly ...

'DEBBIE WILKINS AND ANDY O'BRIEN. Debbie and Andy are living together, they're not married – but it's a serious relationship. The mortgage is in her name ... Debbie is bossy and a planner ... She and her mother decided at an early stage to beat the East-end at its own game, and get Debbie into a different environment ... She wanted to work in a bank and do well ... She became part of a household of six: three women, three men in a huge shared flat in Wandsworth ... Andy used to come over and visit her ... A strange stilted courtship began ... They moved to the square, so Debbie's back in the area that she came from ... Partners, in love, and determined to make it the best home ever – they are not so much acquisitive, as lovers of their comfort ... Her interfering manner upsets other occupants of the square ... Andy knows she has an unfortunate manner and tries to cover for her when he can. Debbie isn't a snob in the social sense, but as she's skilled labour – a professional woman – she's bound to feel sometimes slightly a cut above the others ... Actually, not being accepted by others, being made to feel that they're "outsiders" will frequently prompt Andy and Debbie to consider moving out ... Andy, a Scot, has a very practical contented element in his make-up ... A succession of foster-parents ... He always seemed to be part of families that genuinely wanted him. It's made him very secure, a little smug, perhaps ...? Student Nurse at Glasgow Royal Infirmary ... Unlike Debbie, who's an ambitious woman working in a traditionally male world, Andy is a very unambitious man working in a traditionally female world ... They became in love with the idea that everyone thought they were the perfect couple ... The decision to attempt the experiment of "living together": A "domestic" relationship, was a difficult one, and they agonised over it for months. Wouldn't they get bored? Would they feel imprisoned? How would they fill the hours, with only the two of them? . . . They want to knock down walls, put in double-glazing, and all the rest of it . . . Forced to move into a different class: and that means "up". . . . They're not Habitat/ Guardian East-end, and they're certainly not nouveau-riche, but they are, to a lot of people, a possible sign of the shape of things to come in the Borough . . .'

With only a couple of days left before they exchanged one blustery climate for another, they had brought into being twenty human beings. They had names and addresses, birthdays and jobs, histories and mannerisms, strengths and weaknesses, hopes and secrets.

What they didn't have was the elusive local pub! At present their only meeting-places, apart from the square itself, were the market, the cafe, the launderette and the mini-supermarket. Surely the most important moments in an East-end community's life were acted out in the pub? The local. The boozer . . . Julia and Tony had always been critical of the way pubs were portrayed on television, feeling they lacked vitality and life. They were determined that their pub was going to be the real thing! The idea of putting a 'real' pub on television had been at the back of Tony's mind for many years, since he had worked as a barman. He had found the colourful and exhausting life of the pub-game fascinating, and daily soaked up the sights and sounds, knowing that one day he would need to call on them. Why then had he left this final vital part of the jigsaw, the missing-link, to the last? Maybe because he had already guessed that the pub was going to be a monstrous battleground where emotions, perhaps a little too frightening to think about, were going to shatter the atmosphere like machine-gun fire. Den and Angie, with their helpless daughter, Sharon somewhere in the middle searching for no-man's-land, were going to be a very dramatic couple. If the pub, and the family who lived and worked there, had been invented first, then Julia and Tony might have been too shell-shocked to have created all the other elements.

'JACK, PEARL AND TRACEY WATTS. Jack and Pearl are not criminals. They're not exactly angels either. Villains perhaps? Well, he certainly is. They've been married for fifteen years, and haven't had sex with each other for thirteen of them. The marriage

is a front for the sake of the pub's image. The daughter, Tracey is adopted – maybe for the same reason. They have a dog, too – Prince – an Alsatian ... Pearl met Jack at school, and they were sweethearts from the word go. Money and things are what interest her. Jack didn't give her these fast enough in the early stages of their marriage, which is partly why it turned sour. It also went wrong because of sex: he just didn't turn her on ... or, didn't turn her on enough. And she never stops reminding him of how much a man he isn't. She is basically a scrubber, trying to reform herself. *"Nobody turns me on like Jack,"* she says loudly in public, *"I can't make it with another man."* But she does, often ... "Class" is what Pearl wants, and something she'll never pull off. Yes, she's attractive. She's also *flash* ... Pearl the worker is no fool. She can keep two sets of books with the best of them, hire with skill, and fire without mercy. Sexual innuendo is the key to her character. The wink. The tease ... *"Have you seen his Honda 750? Take me for a ride anytime!"* ... Her pub is spotless. And the customer's always right. Except when he isn't. Then she can be so polite, he'll wish he'd gone to a wine-bar ... Sometimes Pearl gets so legless that Jack has to throw her over his shoulder and fireman's lift her upstairs to their flat, where they have separate bedrooms ... She's fun, she tries and she's trapped. She's also larger than life ... Even with a marriage on the rocks, Jack still likes the area. His mates are here, it's friendly and it's his territory. "Local lad makes good ..." People look up to him. If you've dragged yourself up by the scruff of the neck and moved up a notch, you need a few people around you who didn't quite make it, or you might as well be invisible. He's had a mistress for five years ... Unlike Pearl, she's a very up-market woman, a lady, *real* class. Jack's her bit of rough, and they're happy. They actually talk. With

Fowlers Living Room
Early sketch
'84 two boxes etc.

Kitchen
door

teatray

Biscuit Barrel

photo Mark Fowler

cmo.

The Fowlers' living room. This is Lou Beale's place,—she's lived here from before the war and however much her daughter Pauline and her husband Arthur Fowler would like to change it, they can't. It's a time capsule of Lou's life from her girlhood to her role as matriarch of an East-end family, shown above in a family snapshot taken in the very early days of the show. Mark Fowler (far right of picture) disappeared but his photo remains on the sideboard.

The Beales are a traditional East-end family who have always worked in the market. Lou's husband's barrow is now run by Pete Beale her son, but when Lou's well enough to work it she's better at it than Pete. **Above left:** Pete, Kathy, Lou and Ian Beale. **Left:** The tower block. Pete and Kathy live on the fourteenth floor.

Lou's two grandsons. Wicksy and Ian. Wicksy is an outsider, the first non East-ender to come to Albert Square, but will he turn out to be a part of Pete Beale's past he would rather not know about?

The Queen Vic, focus of so much of the life of Albert
Square, a public house with a public face and a
private one. **Right:** Happy Families: Den Watts with
wife Angie, adopted daughter Sharon and dog Roly,
for once not on the stairs guarding Den's phone. They
may look happy but really they are tearing each other
apart, their conflict providing a continuing dramatic
spine for the show.

glazed oveipeice

hanging pendant

table lamp

Welcome to the Vic, the pub where you'll get everything from a drag show to World War III being played out by the guvnors. It may be night but the lights are blazing *upstairs*—where so much of the action is really taking place.

QV public bar

Check that your vehicle is taxed!

DON'T RISK A HEAVY FINE

THE QUEEN VICTORIA

THE QUEEN VICTORIA

Colin and Barry live in the middle flat at number three Albert Square (red door, right). The two characters' on-screen relationship caused a lot of controversy but demonstrated the show's ability to reflect people's lives as they really live them.

Carmel Roberts, the health visitor and her brother Darren also live at number three, on the first floor.

At the end of 1987 Wicksy and Mags (above) moved in together into the basement flat where the Carpenters had lived.

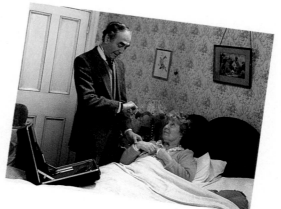

Top: Lofty and Michelle live in dire poverty at the top of number one Albert Square. Is Michelle living too near the Vic where Den is the father of her child and Lofty is his barman? Will Lofty ever find out? **Middle:** Below them lives Ethel who cleans the pub and also cleans Dr Legg's surgery. She is pure old East-end and also the main source of gossip. **Bottom:** In the basement is Dr Legg's surgery, the old style GP who brought most of Albert Square into the world, seen treating Lou Beale at home.

Arthurs Allotment shed

Behind the brick and asphalt of the Square is a little patch of green, Arthur Fowler's allotment. It's all real—when the Elstree gardener isn't planting weeds he's looking after Arthur's vegetables.

Allotment '85

Tons allotment shed

Pearl, you shout – or shut up . . . He's a smart dresser. Changes his shirt twice a day and his shoes sparkle. He runs a good pub. He's firm and fair with the staff. (*"If you've got any problems – go to him, not her."*) The cellars are well organised and spotless. His "masculinity" is the key to his character. It was called into question at an early stage in his marriage and he's defended it ever since. Some call him a ladies' man (because of his good looks) others – a man's man . . . He's a con man and has the gift of the gab. He can defend himself smartly in a brawl. (He's only ever thumped Pearl once.) You can accept Jack being a snob – because it's not malicious: it's done with a grin. Like Pearl – he's also trapped by his background . . . Tracey is at the centre of her parents' dramas. The children of publicans nearly always suffer in one way or another: the fact that your "home" is always "open house" to a variety of strangers often produces genuine feelings of anxiety and insecurity. Tracey, being adopted, will be even more sensitive to this lack of permanence. Jack and Pearl do use her as something of a tennis-ball in their games of playing things off against each other. Jack tries to buy her affection with gifts. Pearl sees her as something of a rival . . . Tracey's set on a course which is almost inevitable. Either, a collision, or, full-circle, to the same route her parents took . . . Jack and Pearl's relationship is pretty heated . . . the smooth public face (workers in pubs are always "on stage"); the trial reconciliations; the rows; the fights and the tears . . . Will Jack ever bring his mistress into the pub, which is Pearl's territory? Will Pearl accept too many free drinks from customers, and, in public, lose control? . . . They were lovers. They are husband and wife. There was affection . . . love . . . if it came to it, could they give each other up? The private grins and winks to each other when they're working as a team – which usually means taking money. The love turning to hatred . . . Jack-the-lad and the artificial pearl . . . They're an electric couple . . .'

Twenty-three characters in search of an author had finally come home to roost. The amazing thing they discovered when they read through their 'biographies' was that they had not just invented a group of characters, they had created an entire community as well, with connections and links stretching right back into everyone's past lives. Pete must have known Jack (soon to become Den) at school. Maybe they had met Tony in the playground as well, perhaps they were the very ones who had given him the racial abuse? Did Pearl (soon to become Angie) know Sue and Kathy at school, or Pete's first wife, Pat? Surely Den and Pete, after all this time, would have become good mates? And if Arthur was someone that Pauline had 'known from school' then they must all have run into each other as schoolkids. (Just as Mark, Michelle, Ian, Kelvin and Tracey – soon to become Sharon – would do in the next generation . . .) Lou would have known Ethel's husband, William, and Ethel Lou's husband, Albert. And Doctor Legg would know the full history of everyone, as he probably brought most of them into the world! Minds were overdosing on words, fingers were numb with the constant scribbling and backs were breaking from leaning too far forward over the typewriter. Time to declare an interval, a brief pause to let the air out of the balloon. But that was a luxury they could not afford. There was still that overall story-plan to construct, and the detailed story-lines, the start of what were to be the first twenty episodes.

Re-reading those original biographies (which was to become a weekly ritual) gave them some pointers about possible long-term plans. What in particular jumped off the pages and demanded to be explored over fairly long periods of time?

'Pauline was also pregnant' . . . 'Arthur was made redundant and has been unemployed for a year' . . . 'Michelle is obviously more on the straight and narrow' . . . 'Pete's two sons by his first marriage are nineteen and twenty and he hardly sees them' . . . 'Pete's first wife was a vicious shrew' . . . 'Maybe if Tony and Hannah split, they could find themselves again?' . . . 'Sue and Ali have a nine-month son named after Ali's dad: Hassan. And they're devoted to him' . . . 'Den's "masculinity" is the key to his character' . . . 'Will Den ever bring his mistress into the pub, which is Angie's territory?' . . . 'If it came to it, could Den and Angie give each other up?' . . .

A sequence of forward storylines was starting to take shape. Pauline would have her baby, which would add to the already considerable problems of overcrowding in that tiny little council house. At the same time she would have to remain the lynchpin of the family, as Lou's health deteriorated, and Arthur's depression about being unemployed increased. (If Arthur's inability to get a job continues, it could start affecting his mental state, and possibly climax in some sort of nervous breakdown.) Michelle would not stay on the straight and narrow for long. A little way into the serial she would become pregnant. (The drama and problems of a schoolgirl pregnancy is something Julia and Tony had wanted to explore for a long time. Of course, Sharon's the obvious character to get pregnant. But why go for the obvious?) Question is, who's the father of Michelle's baby? (Better leave the answer to that one until the autumn of '85 – when the audience is at its highest. That ought to keep a hold on the viewers then, through to the new year!) That means four babies in the show, Mary's, Pauline's, Michelle's and Sue and Ali's! How could the studio cope with four babies? One of them would have to go. Mary's baby perhaps, to Stockport to her parents? Or Sue and Ali's (There had been a lot in the papers recently about an increase in the number of cot deaths. And a certain doctor had upset a lot of people by appearing to suggest that the reason could be something to do with the parents. Maybe they could put the record straight on that one? It was a harrowing subject whatever, but if they handled it carefully, researched it thoroughly . . . If they didn't sensationalise it they were sure it could work.) Hannah, plus the other child (a girl perhaps?) must come back into Tony's life 'for the sake of the family' – but not stay around for too long because the neighbourhood would appal her. (Tie in with Debbie's attitude to the East-end?) Will Tony search for his real roots back in Trinidad? Den, of course, will be the father of Michelle's baby, and the child will be his first too. (Sharon's adopted, remember?) It is important that only Michelle, Den and the audience know this fact, then every time any reference is made, they will feel they're party to a very special secret. Den's mistress should turn up at the pub, under her own steam (Christmas '85, or New Year, maybe? to try and consolidate whatever audience the show has by then . . .) See Den surrounded by all his women, Angie, Sharon, 'mistress' and now Michelle for at least a year! Fearing that Den might ditch her at any moment, Angie should try everything in her power to keep him. They should divorce, Christmas 1986. (Need something for the '86 autumn 'hook', though. Wedding? Michelle's?) Then spend at least another year getting Den and Angie back together again, autumn '87. And what about the Christmas/New Year '87/'88 cliffhanger? Kill someone off?

They'd moved, at breakneck speed, from January 1985 to January 1988. Three years?! Would East 8 survive that long? Would it manage three weeks? Forget about it, that sort of thing was for audiences and planners on the sixth floor to worry about . . .

A framework of criss-cross lines was now down on paper in black and white, outlining some of the major events that might occur with the peaks timed to take full advantage of the audience potential, assuming it was there. Now came the job of reading between those lines, adding the colours, the light and shade, to make the canvas complete.

They wanted to tell the audience right from the beginning that there were certain things they should learn to expect from East 8. Firstly, it was *not* going to beat about the bush. If they wanted a cosy, meandering journey through never-never land then this was not going to be the show for them, and they ought to have that fact pointed out to them from the beginning. The show's location was a rough one, violent even. But there was a strong sense of community. Also a unique sense of humour, that might take them an episode or two to get used to. It was also very much about families and relationships. It was going to be fast-moving, tough, and firmly rooted in the 'eighties, set uncompromisingly in Thatcher's Britain.

Julia Smith and Tony Holland decided to start episode one with a bang! – to make sure everyone knew they meant business.

EPISODE ONE

'East 8 starts with a bang, as a size ten boot kicks down a door that's locked from the inside. The tiny, dirty and foul-smelling council-flat behind the battered door belongs to Reg Cox (known locally as "the-old-boy", and a cantankerous bastard at the best of times) who hasn't been seen round the square for days . . . Once the door's down, three men rush into the gloomy main-room: Den, the publician, Arthur and Ali, the Turkish Cypriot – still in his pyjamas or dressing-gown. They find the old boy sitting in his favourite armchair beside the gas-fire (which isn't on) – and he's very nearly dead . . .

'Shouts of "Hypothermia", "Don't touch him", "Get an ambulance . . ." By the end of the episode the old boy will have been removed from the square and taken to Intensive Care, and

the entire community will be rife with gossip, which spreads
round the houses like the plague.

'Via the gossip we're able to piece together the events leading
up to the discovery of Reg. Saeed and Naima, at the mini-
supermarket, were the first to remark on Reg Cox's absence: he
hadn't been in for his half pint of milk for days. A casual remark
to Den and Pete, and Pauline, at the launderette, sparked off a
general enquiry round the square. *"Had anyone seen Reg . . .?"* No
reply from Reg's front-door bell, so Ali (in the flat below) was
woken up. Had he seen Reg about? No, he hadn't. And there's
a couple of letters for Reg in the hall, dated days ago. So – the
decision is made to force an entry.

'Gossip starts in the pub, via Den, Angie and Ethel. *"Whatever
happened to community spirit? Kinship? This would never have
happened in the 'old days',"* etc. (Start to indicate the relationship
between Den and Angie, and plant that it's their wedding
anniversary.)

'Gossip moves to the launderette: via Pauline, Arthur and
maybe Lou. (Later, leaving her mum to cover for her at the
launderette, or when the second shift woman has taken over,
Pauline goes to the surgery. Doctor Legg and Pauline are both
happy about the fact that she's pregnant. He'd be even happier
if she lost a bit of weight and stopped smoking. He'd be happier
still if Pauline would summon up the courage to break the "good
news" to her mum.)

'The gossip continues in the street market (establish that Pete
and Den are good mates) and to the tea-bar . . . Ali and Sue are
starting to get a bit uptight: they live in the same house as the
old boy and people are beginning to suggest that as they were
nearest they should have been better neighbours, and realised
something. Aggro starts between Sue and Kathy.

'Saeed and Naima are probably feeling a bit proud and
community-conscious about the whole incident, because they
were the ones who initiated the enquiries. (Establish their
inexperience in the shop, and the fact that his parents have only
just returned to India.)

'Biggest event is Pauline and Arthur breaking the news to Lou
about Pauline's pregnancy. Lou goes bonkers! How could they
be so stupid? Or, how could Arthur be so stupid? There's already
five of them in a tiny council house – how are they going to cope

plaster
decoration
to door
surround
Public
Bar

Keith Harris begins to flesh in the Queen Vic with exterior detail. Because the show is recorded seven weeks in advance turning spring into early summer, keeping the trees in Albert Square in step with the seasons requires the addition of extra foliage.

caps to pilaster / Stock Wale
plaster w/shop

plaster cornice

VICTORIA

etched glass

hanging baskets

Saloon

garden shrubs + trees

pavement

Railings / metal workers.

with a sixth? And, where's the money coming from to feed the extra mouth? Lou reminds Arthur, brutally, that he's out of work ... *"And because of this bloody ruction, I've missed me Bingo!"* In the middle of the family row – Michelle and Mark arrive home from school.

'Kathy arrives at the pub to "open up". Den, in shirt sleeves, checks she's okay, then goes upstairs to get ready. Reg Cox is still the main topic of conversation downstairs. Ali is in the "Public" – playing darts probably for money ... He can hear all the chat – the innuendo ... *"If only people had been good neighbours like they used to be in the old days the old boy would be all right ..."* Sue blows, and has a screaming-match with Kathy. Ali blows! He starts a punch-up that gets so bloody and violent that Kathy's forced to ring the emergency bell for the "Guvnor" to come down. Den leaps over the bar, separates the fighters, and they're "barred" ... And one of them puts his fist through the pub window ...'

EPISODE TWO

"Bloody great wedding-anniversary this is going to turn out to be," says Den. *"There's already been a punch-up in the Public."*

'We are upstairs at the pub: observing Den and Angie when they are not "on stage" behind the bar. The chat is about Den wanting to get rid of the "Public", turning the pub into one bar. Angie, meanwhile, couldn't care, she wants to go up-market and move away from the area altogether, but Den would rather remain and stay a big fish in a small pool. Most of the talk is about money. Business is the worst it's been for years. Is the bottom falling out of the pub game? See Den, the villain. *"Don't wear that shirt tonight. It was on Police Five last Sunday."* *"Get your second set of books out, darlin'. I'm going down the cut-price tomorrow. Get us a couple of cases of whisky – special offer ..."* We meet Sharon for the first time. Piggy in the middle ... Angie makes her first crack about Den not being a proper man ... And then we contrast the upstairs "private life", with the downstairs "public life" which seems all sweetness and light, husband and wife, daughter and dog family ... Even so, Den manages to telephone his mistress and get in a bit of mild flirtation with Kathy: *"I thought my old man was your best mate ...?"* Contrast

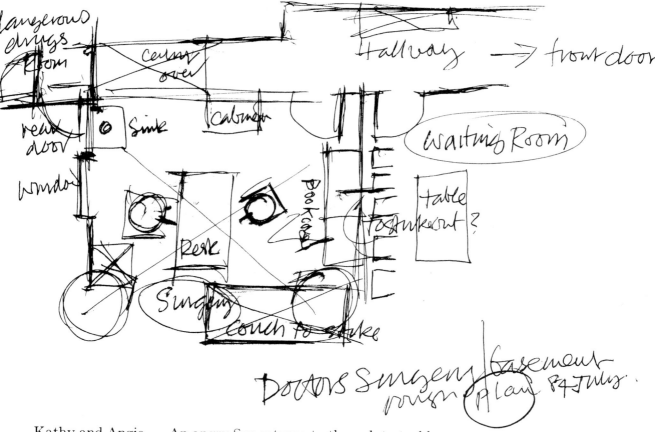

Labels in sketch: dangerous drugs Room · cellar over · Hallway → front door · rear door · Sink · Cabinet · Waiting Room · table · Door Room · Trunk room? · window · Desk · Surgery · couch to strike · Doctors Surgery Basement rough Plan 84 July.

Series Designer's rough plan dated July 84 of Dr Legg's surgery.

Kathy and Angie ... An angry Sue returns to the pub to tackle Angie and Den about her Ali being barred. *"It's because he's a Cypriot ..."* etc. At the end of the evening Angie is legless, and Den has to fireman's lift her upstairs ...

'Pauline and Arthur turn up at the pub too, after the continuing row at home about the "baby". Both Michelle and Mark are home by now, and Arthur knows she'll go spare if they don't get out. At the pub we learn that they both want the child. It's basically a happy, slightly sentimental scene. But Arthur drinks too much, he doesn't want to go home to face the cruel "old bag" Lou. Pauline has to go home so asks sister-in-law Kathy, behind the bar, to keep an eye on him. Arthur ends up spending the night on the settee at Pete and Kathy's flat in the tower-block, and he tells them the good news about the baby.

'Morning after the night before. Ethel cleans Doctor's surgery. *"How's Reg?" "Still unconscious."*

'Ali, the malingerer, visits Doctor Legg – he's hurt himself during the punch-up at the pub. Overdoes it. Not allowed to work. (Tea-bar *or* minicab driving.) (Keep going throughout the gossip about Ali and Sue not being the best of neighbours ... and let's see some of Sue's bitchery coming to the surface, e.g. she decides to bar Kathy and Pete from the tea-bar.)

'Tail between his legs, Arthur turns up at the launderette and market. *"Go and make your peace with Lou. Buy her a box of chocs."* Arthur borrows the money from Pete, and buys the chocolates from the mini-supermarket. But, when he confronts Lou, she stubbornly digs her heels in: *"Either you have the kiddie adopted, get rid of it, or you get out of my house. The whole lot of you!"*

'Ethel, cleaning at the pub, will probably be a bit amused watching Angie trying to cope with a massive hangover. And Den, getting the lunchtime rolls from the tea-bar, will have to come face to face with Ali since barring him from the pub. Den tries to talk Angie through the alterations he would like to do in the pub. Angie's not really interested. Wants a "better" pub. Round to the subject of "money" again.

'Shortly before lunchtime closing, Den goes off to the cut-price place to pick up his cases of whisky. And that's the moment the Area Manager from the brewery decides to pay a visit. Angie posts Ethel outside the pub to look out for Den and instructs her to tell him not to bring the booze into the pub. Angie closes the pub and offers the Area Manager a drink – "on the house", of course. When Den returns, shiftily, to the pub, there's no Ethel. She's been distracted somewhere, fortune-telling in the market perhaps. And so, Den, case of whisky in his arms (not a brand supplied by the brewery) charges into the saloon bar, and comes face to face with the Area Manager.

'Reg Cox, in hospital, dies. And his death is being treated as murder . . .'

Two down, eighteen to go! Making up the first twenty detailed storylines was harder than they thought it would be. They had to become jugglers. In order to keep East 8 punchy and fast-moving, they had to have several stories going on simultaneously, which meant keeping lots of balls in the air at the same time. It was so easy to get bogged down with one string and lose the thread of another. Just as it was so easy to lose track of the people. The residents of the Square were still brand new to Julia and Tony, had only just been brought into life and carrying all twenty-three of them in their heads at once, was not simple.

'. . . Mary was to arrive in the Square and move into Reg Cox's old room – the room of a dead man. (Establish Social Worker,

Mary's inability to read and write, lack of a job, lack of money)
... Den will con Angie into letting him have a holiday on his
own in Spain. In fact he's going to be with his mistress, at her
villa. (Keep Dan's mistress as an off-stage presence for as long
as possible. The telephone in the downstairs corridor in the pub
must represent her. Whenever it rings the audience's first
thought must be that it might be her) ... Angie will discover the
truth about Den's deception, and have a brief fling with Tony.
(He must take it seriously and end up very hurt) ... Michelle and
Sharon are to become rivals for Kelvin, Sharon even going so far
as to offer to go on the ''pill'' for him. (Mary Whitehouse isn't
going to like this! But, as both sides of the debate will be aired,
there's not a lot she can say, really, but, knowing her, she'll
probably still say it! Actually, the story could give a lot of very
useful information. Get people talking) ... At the Fowlers, Lou
will develop shingles. Pauline will be put under such pressure
that she will collapse from exhaustion and be rushed into hospital.
(She won't lose the baby. Don't want to frighten pregnant forty-
year-olds) ... The Council will announce plans to demolish one
side of the Square and sell the land to property developers. A
''Save the Square'' campaign will start, involving Legg, Debs,
Andy, Saeed and Naima. (Interesting how the different classes
are already putting themselves into neat little ghettos) ... The
mini-supermarket will be broken into (NF graffiti on doors –
menace) and Naima will crash into Ali's minicab when Saeed's
giving her a driving-lesson ...'

With what seemed like seconds before the coach was to arrive
to drive them back to the airport, they had finished what they'd
set out to do. The biographies ran to forty pages. The overall
story-plan to fifteen. And the detailed storylines to forty-five. One
hundred pages in all! Three hundred words had been transformed
into thirty thousand.

Inevitably, the sun came out, as they were boarding the plane.
The aircraft reached 30,000 feet in only minutes. It had taken
Julia and Tony slightly longer to reach the same number of
words. Just before they dozed off, they vowed never to return to
Lanzarote. In months to come the very mention of its name would
bring them out in a cold sweat.

LONDON BOROUGH OF WALFORD

ALBERT SQUARE

E20

Please make up 4 London Square signs as
indicated — in metal — Required before Nov 84

Making it Happen

22 March, 1984. Somewhere over southern Spain, the devisers of East 8 were woken up by a smiling woman dressed in red, white and blue, and presented with plastic trays of lunch. They ordered Bucks Fizz to take away the taste of the food, and the champagne set them buzzing again. They decided that when they got 'home', they would put the biogs and the storylines aside for a week and forget all about them, then when they picked them up again, they would be looking with a fresh eye, and would be more able to spot mistakes, holes and inconsistencies. Next they had to turn their attention to scripts, which means choosing writers. They had already opted to commission the scripts in groups of four, and for the first batch they wanted to select writers they know, who they have worked with before. People they were comfortable with, who understood their working methods, and who they could trust. They chose Jane Hollowood and Valerie Georgeson from 'Angels', and Bill Lyons who had contributed to just about every show that Tony's ever worked on. But, who should be the fourth? Surely, it ought to be a Londoner? A genuine East-ender who knows the patch like the back of his hand. But where to find such a person? They decided to leave the fourth slot open for the moment.

Julia returned to her house in Chiswick and Tony to his flat in Shepherds Bush, both of them worn out. Then the phone started, with a ring that seemed shriller than usual. Probably because they haven't heard a telephone for fourteen days.

'Did you get everything done? Are you happy with it? Elstree's going fine . . . the Lot's coming on in leaps and bounds. What was the weather like? Are you brown?

23 March, 1984. Audience-research wanted a page or two about what East 8 was going to be about, and a breakdown of the proposed main characters to try out on samples of people up and down the land. Just a paragraph each, please . . .

29 March, 1984. Julia and Tony re-read the biographies and the storylines. Anticipating disaster, they were pleasantly surprised to discover that they held up well and that feeling of 'a whole community' came across even stronger than before. Everything was 'polished', re-typed and sent off to the previously chosen three writers. (Writer number four still had not materialised.) The first Writers' meeting was to be in seven days time.

3 April, 1984. The second report from audience-research became available, with the general public's first reaction to the concept and setting of the show and their thoughts on some of the main characters. On the strength of four group meetings held in London and the outskirts of Manchester, it appeared that when people thought of the East-end and cockneys they thought of a 'quickly witty and dry sense of humour. Hostile in a way, yet friendly.' They imagined people to be kind, territorial and have close families. The image of the Pearly King and Queen still prevailed and they guessed the programme would be overflowing with rogues, tarts, villains and gossips – all of whom would have hearts of gold. They felt it essential that the characters should hate, despise and love: 'goody-goodies' would be too bland. They wanted good scripts, sets and acting – 'Coronation Street in the South'.

As for the characters, although the older people interviewed reacted favourably to Lou, generally it was agreed that it wasn't possible to 'see' the matriarchal family. And the groups were very concerned about 'poor Arthur' ... They insisted that Den had to be a villain, and they reckoned Angie was great. But they were worried that Den and Angie's unhappy relationship would be 'too like home'. Ethel – who they felt would clean and 'do' for people – could possibly be eccentric, and vague, but on no account was she to be 'looney'. Debbie and Andy wouldn't fit in at all!

Young people were thrilled there were to be teenagers – 'No other soap does that!' And Doctor Legg would become the most favourite character of all. *'He can go into everybody's houses – and the ladies would be after him.'* Though some were perturbed about 'medical ethics'.

Julia and Tony decided that the findings were all very interesting but that if they pay any attention to them they will have to fly back to Lanzarote and start all over again!

Cecily Ware, a writers' agent, called Tony, upset that she had not got one of her writers onto the first team for East 8. She'd been hoping that Tony would consider Gerry Huxham, a Londoner, whom he'd met briefly back in the days of Z Cars. Tony decided to risk it. Could Gerry be at the office tomorrow at 10.00? They'll send the biogs and the storylines by car tonight.

4 April, 1984. The first writers' meeting. Had they got the mix of personalities right? Gerry Huxham, the last writer to be chosen, was also the last to arrive. Thirty minutes late, in fact, a habit he was to turn into a routine over the coming months. You could set your watches by him. Even devious little ploys, like telling him the meetings were half an hour earlier than intended, did nothing to improve his time-keeping. East 8 learned to live with it, and blamed it on artistic temperament. Gerry is short (as is his hair), stocky, sartorially dapper (red braces) and rolls his own cigarettes. His humour is sometimes disconcerting. Is he being funny, serious or just taking the mick? He was to prove invaluable to the show, he knew London from 'the inside', was not backward in coming forward and must take a lot of the credit for not letting things get 'cosy'.

Jane Hollowood seemed positively 'county' in comparison, rural to Gerry's urban. Tall, sleek, with long black hair and long black clothes to match, Jane is fiercely intelligent, and possesses that enviable ability to be able to get right inside a character and know exactly how they will speak.

Valerie Georgeson is also tall and slim, and usually wears pretty floral-print dresses. (If Jane was Autumn, then Val was definitely Spring!) Valerie is more excitable that the others, more nervy perhaps, and the strength of her writing lies in her knack of latching-on to big emotions, and big issues. She's a vegetarian, and seems to be allergic to everything under the sun, including the allergy-bracelet she wears on her wrist. Her vegetarianism is shared by the final writer, Bill Lyons.

Bill, with long shaggy hair falling over his shoulders (looking just like the world had stopped some time in the 'sixties), is a heavy smoker and a self-confessed 'hack', referring to himself as 'only a jobbing writer, Guv'. Would that one could find a million or two like him! His passion for 'social issues' and defence of the 'underdog' shine through his work like a searchlight. He also has an unmalicious sense of humour that pervades every aspect of his writing, and his dialogue is taut and spare, and bang up to date.

Here were four individuals, seemingly poles apart, but Julia and Tony were hoping that they also had one thing in common, a longing to communicate their various talents to a large audience.

The meeting kicked off, with Tony as coach, and Julia as referee. The writers responded positively to most of the character-biographies, needing only a minimum of clarification of a few fine points. They thought some characters did not quite come off the

Queen Vic door detail.

page and hit you between the eyes and others they felt were slightly obscure. One or two they reckoned to be completely dead. The devisers tried to defend their 'babies', but it was obvious there was still a lot of work to do. At this stage, the writers started to contribute ideas and thoughts of their own. Slowly, they began to re-shape some of the people, influencing their development and behaviour. Ideas were leapt on, or rejected and this process took many hours. It was vitally important that everyone in that room had an identically clear picture of what these faceless individuals were like, as they would have to write for them in the dark. Where did Den meet his mistress, and what was her name? What GCEs would Kelvin be taking? What was Sharon's reaction to her parents sleeping in different rooms? If Naima's shop was to be open-fronted, wouldn't she freeze to death in just a sari? Just as a particular character seemed to have finally taken shape, someone would chip in with: *'No, I'm sorry – I still can't **see** her. Tell me about her again.'*

And so it went on . . . Tony noted the suggestions, now arriving thick and fast, and would later have to weave them into the existing framework, ready for the next meeting. Because of the adjustments to characters a lot of the original stories would now have to be altered, so there seemed little point in going on to discuss the storylines. Anyway, discussions had already eaten in to so much of the day that it was getting late. Time to call it a day? But, no! The writers wanted to keep the meeting going. East 8 was becoming clearer to them and they didn't want to lose it. As far as the storylines were concerned, the meeting never got beyond the first query raised. All four writers wanted to know one thing, and they had all come up with the same question independently – who had killed Reg Cox? Julia and Tony were dumbfounded. They had no idea who'd killed Reg Cox. The who was not important. The fact that he was dead, probably after a violent assault, did matter. Reg's murder was not intended to be solved, it was only there to tell the audience, from the outset, that East 8's location was rough and tough. They were accused by the writers of cheating, and throwing away the possibility for drama that a murder hunt would provide. All the regular characters could be suspects, and a police investigation, with house-to-house enquiries, would be the ideal device for introducing the audience to all the residents of the Square. Tony and Julia promised to give the sugggestion serious consideration, and brought the meeting to a close.

All six retired to 'Albertine' and East 8 was temporarily shelved. Except that it wasn't for Julia and Tony (and for the first of many times they heard themselves thinking, 'Is there life after the bi-weekly?') for they knew that the writers had hit an important nail on the head. Who *did* kill Reg Cox? They did a hasty mental flick through their list of characters. Was there a potential killer on it? No there wasn't. They would have to invent one. Create a new biography to add to the growing collection of others, and then filter him into the storylines. Nick Cotton was born.

The gang-of-four's next meeting with the 'Guvnors' wasn't to be until 17 May. In the meantime, the writers were to make private field trips to the East-end to soak up, and retain in their heads, as much of the rich atmosphere as they could. Once the show was ready to go there would be no time for such luxuries.

May, 1984. While the writers did their own thing, Tòny (now officially off 'Cold Warrior' and allowed to have his own secretary) created Nick Cotton.

'. . . his image is exclusively macho. Vanishes for weeks on end. Mum doesn't ask questions . . . Unlike Den, Nick is a real crook. Worms his way into people's confidentiality and homes. From then on, lives on his wits. Waiting for the moment to strike; to nick the cash and disappear . . . usually chooses his victims who, for one reason or another, are frightened to report him . . . Nick's a heroin addict . . .'

Tony then revised the biographies and the storylines and met writer after writer; it was clear he was going to need a battalion of them. Julia pressed on with yet more meetings, in spite of the fact that she was starting to lose her voice. There were meetings with Equity, the actors' trade union about conditions for the cast, meetings with the Copyright Department and the Writers' Guild over terms and conditions for the show's writers. There were conferences with publicity over appointing the show its own press officer, something that had never been done before.

And, while Tony interviewed his authors, so Julia started hunting out possible directors. She was going to need a list as long as your arm. Up to now only one had been approached, Matthew Robinson. He had enormous experience of working in fast turn-

Queen Vic interior detail.
The 'ex-brewery' beer
pumps actually work in the
set as finally built.

pumps at brewery

graphics.

Saloon Bar

round popular drama, and had already worked with them on 'Angels' . . .

17 May, 1984. The second meeting of the gang of four. They had already been sent the updated material, and were very happy with the 'who-dun-it' strand. And they all agreed that Nick Cotton was going to be a splendidly nasty character to write for. It was considered wise not to start the ball rolling by writing episodes one and two first. Much better to leave that important pair till later when a programme style might have been discovered. So, Gerry, Jane, Val and Bill would be writing episodes three to six between them, but not till the end of the meeting would they know which specific episode was to be theirs. The four revised storylines were worked through paragraph by paragraph, then line by line. And more changes were made, additions, subtractions, multiplications and divisions. And fresh problems were found, to be ironed out and corrected. Hours later the meeting was satisfied that the four outlines were as near perfect as they would ever be. So – who was writing which . . .?

Suddenly the office turned into bedlam as a free-for-all was declared. A system was initiated at that meeting that was to become forever a tradition. Basically, what it amounted to, was that the writers had to fight for the episode they wanted. (Later on, writers were to turn the proceedings into open warfare, mainly of the psychological variety. They bargain, tease and play terrible games with each other. *'I definitely want to write the second episode!'* often means: *'That's the one episode I don't want to write. But, if I fight hard enough for it, one of the other writers might be fooled into thinking it's the best!'* Bluff, and double-bluff. More often than not, writers and episodes are paired without much trouble. But just occasionally, a writer is lumbered with a storyline they either

don't like or don't think is very good. In which case, the meeting
continues until that writer *is* happy. The episode in question is
pulled to pieces once more, put under the microscope, patched,
bolstered and analysed to such an extent that it usually ends up
the best storyline of the four!)

The creative part of the session is now over, it's down to the
logistics. How many 'cast' in each episode for example. Restric-
tions on budget force this consideration on the team. How many
'sets', and which ones? (Amount of studio space dictates this.
Keith Harris, with Julia and Tony, has already decided which
sets will be permanently standing at one end of the studio. But
at the other end there can be three other sets, taken from a pool
of many. The writers have to agree which ones their stories need.
And once chosen, they have to stick to them!) Phone numbers are
exchanged, and the writers depart. By three o' clock the next day,
they must have dictated by phone their version of their storyline
to Tony's secretary. If their outline is OK, the day after that they
can start writing. And two weeks after that they must deliver two
copies of the finished script.

Tony and Julia had first been approached about doing the
BBC's new soap in March, 1983. Now, fourteen months later,
some scripts were actually going to be written. In another two
weeks, there would be something to read.

But, in two weeks, Julia would not be there. She would be in
Italy, in the modern spa town of Chianciano, some thirty minutes'
drive north of Rome. Along with programme-makers from tele-
vision companies all over Europe, she was a delegate at the
European Broadcasting Union's conference on 'Popular Drama'.
This was high-powered stuff!

Bill Podmore, the Executive Producer of 'Coronation Street',
was there, as was the recently appointed (and soon to be written
out?) producer of 'Crossroads'. 'Brookside' was represented and
'Pobol y cwm' the Welsh soap. And Fleet Street was in evidence
too, with TV journalists from the *Guardian* and the *Daily Express*.
It's not often that professional television people, a lot of them
rivals for the same audience, get the opportunity to meet and
share common interests and concerns. And, at that 1984 conference, the concerns about the state of European television were
enormous. Cheaply bought American programmes were flooding
the home market and threatening to wipe it out. It was suggested

by one delegate that the only truly European programme was 'Dallas', as it occupied the same high position in the ratings in every single country. And with the arrival of cable and satellite, there was a real danger that European television services would wither away, and that separate national identities would be replaced by bland, homogenised pap. If they were to survive, there was an urgent need for popular, 'cheap' but forceful, quality European drama. The threat from America had to be faced head-on. The conference was a chance for people from different countries, united by the fact that they were all part of Europe, to swap notes about how their different programmes got to the screen, and maybe also to learn something from those notes.

Subject matter, techniques, costings, these were the things under consideration, the nuts and bolts of getting popular drama on the screen and winning an audience, mundane perhaps but vitally important. It was also an opportunity to make new professional contacts, and consolidate old ones. Julia, the 'new girl' at the conference, had decided in advance to maintain a low profile. She didn't have a completed programme (or even a completed script!) to show anyone, and anyway wanted East 8 kept firmly under wraps. Swapping professional niceties was one thing, but giving away ideas was something else. All anyone knew about East 8 was that it was going to be transmitted twice a week, early evening, and was set in London's East-end. And if Julia was discreet that's all they ever would know. But discretion (particularly about story-ideas!) didn't prevent a healthy exchange of knowledge and expertise, and the forming of some sound friendships. Some of these friendships would be tested to the limit when in the months to come the 'Battle of the Soaps' was invented by the popular press. Julia formed a cautious admiration for Bill Podmore from the 'Street'. They spoke the same language. Their programmes even had the same budget. What they didn't speak about was the fact that their shows would be chasing the same audience. Bill invited Julia to Manchester, when she got back to England, to look at the set for 'Coronation Street' and also to visit the location for his new soap opera (or 'Folk Opera' as he dubbed it), due to reach the screens at about the same time as East 8.

A *new* bi-weekly?! Something to do with a 'market'. A market! Julia didn't panic, or if she did she managed to conceal it. What about their market in East 8? Would the two programmes be treading on each other's toes? Which one would be on the screens first? Should she and Tony consider dropping their market? Better to forget anything drastic until more information could be found out about this new show. Julia had decided to tag a few days' holiday (the last for at least a year) onto the end of the conference, and motor over to the Italian east coast. But before she left, and almost in the middle of saying her 'farewells', another bombshell landed in her lap. A new Controller of BBC-1 had been appointed, Michael Grade. Julia had never met him, but, like everyone else, had picked up vibes about his reputation and style on the TV grapevine. He was rumoured to be young, dynamic and 'commercial'. What would a change of Controller mean for East 8?

As Julia drove off on her brief holiday, a chance remark of Bill Podmore's kept nagging in her ears: *'You do realise,'* he'd said, *'that if East 8 is a success, your life will be taken over, and things will never be the same again . . .?'*

June, 1984. The 'Battle of the Soaps' began sooner than anyone expected. On 2 June, an article 'from James Murray in Italy' appeared in the *Daily Express*, likening Julia and Bill Podmore to a couple of army-generals from opposing camps, soon to engage in bloody combat. Combat that was to be a fight to the death. It was starting.

Julia arrived back in England full of the 'market' project that Bill Podmore was doing for Granada. (Tony had heard from a private source that it was going to be about an 'enclosed' market, not a street market. Fingers were kept heavily crossed, that the two programmes would not cover the same ground.) She was also excited to know how the scripts were progressing. As much as one can be certain of anything in uncharted waters, the scripts appeared to be in good nick, and shaping-up nicely. There had been a few teething problems, as there always were, but nothing to get alarmed about. The very different and original styles of the four writers had been the first hiccup. There was no cohesion, each episode had come over as a separate item, more like a one-off play than part of a continuing drama. And their perception of some of the characters was at odds too. Sue Osman was too overtly bitchy in one script, yet not bitchy enough in another. The teenagers were too young in Valerie's episode, too old in Bill's. Jane seemed

The building of Phase One of the permanent set, the first three sides of the square, took place through the summer of 1984.
Above: The pub approaches completion.
Left: Topping out with fibreglass chimney pots. Meanwhile the pub, even the square itself, didn't have names.

nervous of making Lou an 'old bag', Gerry had made her into a monster! But during Julia's absence, Tony had met the writers separately and prodded and pushed, nurtured and guided, and their second drafts were looking good.

Work at Elstree proceeded on two fronts. The construction of the actual square, on the outside Lot, and the rebuilding and refurbishment of the working environment. Tony continued his

Simon Supertunes Ltd.

c.c. Julia Smith
Alan Jeapes
Bruce Talbot
S. M.

				TIME
E8.				
OPENING TITLES.	MONO. NON-DOLBY 15 IPS	(M1)	SOFT FINISH	33 secs.
		(M2) (A)	QUICK END WITHOUT ECHO END	24 secs ✱
		(B)	WITH ECHO END	25 secs ✱
END TITLES		(M3)	TOMS START	1-35
		(M4)	SAME AS M3 WITHOUT TOMS START	1-33
	20 secs + 1-33 secs. →	(M5)	COCKNEY START	1-33
		(M6)	ROMANTIC PRE-EMPT	20 sec + 1-33
		(M7)	LONGEST VERSION	1-54
FULL VERSIONS IN STEREO commercial recording		(M8)	A SIDE	
		(M9)	B SIDE	

✱ n.b. (M2)(A) was what you heard in the studio. (M2)(B) is exactly the same, but with slight echo added at the end which we prefer. You can decide!!

search for prospective writers, by now almost giving up hope of finding that elusive breed, a genuine East-end writer. Julia meanwhile pushed on with her search for directors. She had chosen the first three.

27 June, 1984. At a meeting for all producers and script-editors, Jonathan Powell, after first welcoming the appointment of Michael Grade as Controller, BBC-1, announced what would be the department's output for the coming year. He left mention of East 8 till the very end, but then proceeded to give it the hardest sell possible, stressing its importance to the Corporation, and its need of support and encouragement from everyone in the department. (Rumours about opposing attitudes to the soap had obviously filtered through to him.)

Glad of the chance to remove themselves for a while from the world of words, Julia and Tony turned their attention to music and pictures. East 8 had to have opening and closing titles and a theme tune. This was difficult to get right at the best of times, but even harder on a programme that would be entering the country's living-rooms twice a week, every week of the year, for God knows how long. The titles and music would have only a few seconds to precisely capture the essence of the show. And they would have to do this without ever boring the audience. Tony had been very impressed by the combined talents of Simon May, composer, and Alan Jeapes, graphic-designer, who between them had concocted the titles and music for 'Cold Warrior'. Independently they were both highly skilled craftsmen, in tandem, they were something else! They met them both, and outlined their conception of the programme, something which by now was almost a daily routine. 'Jeapes' puffed on a cigar and went away for a think. Simon, demo-tape, Walkman and two sets of headphones at the ready, was back in what seemed like minutes, with a theme for them to listen to. They didn't like it. It was a pleasant enough tune, but it didn't convey London. It didn't conjure up 'stiff-upper-lipped cockneys', the sounds of Bow Bells were nowhere to be heard, it didn't have a 'whistle' and it said nothing about the fact that the East-end was multi-racial. Simon is not the sort of person to give up easily, and shortly he returned with his second attempt.

This had the lot! Bells, whistles, hand-claps, sitars, steel-drums

Left: The original memo from Simon May laying out details of the 'E8' theme tune. All the various versions of the EastEnders theme tune were chosen at this early stage. The 'romantic pre-empt' was used first in Episode 66 featuring Michelle and Den in the final shot. The 'Cockney Start' featuring a barrel organ has never been used on screen.

and an underlying feeling of being on a merry-go-round. It also had an hypnotic melody which Julia and Tony found themselves humming along to after only one hearing. The usually painful process of choosing music for a programme had been accomplished without so much as a scratch. A copy of the tape was sent to Jeapes, and for the next week, three crazy people could be seen wandering the BBC's corridors, humming and whistling Simon's mesmeric theme. Sometimes Julia, mid-hum, would burst into Tony's office: *'I've forgotten the middle bit! Whistle the middle bit!'* Other members of staff decided that the programme was finally getting to them.

Alan Jeapes was going through what he describes as his 'maps' phase (the opening titles of 'Cold Warrior' had featured a map of Russia) and he'd come up with an idea for East 8 that was incredibly simple, and therefore had a chance of standing up to the test of time. He wanted a black-and-white aerial view of the whole of the East-end. A bird's (cockney sparrow's?) eye view that was revealed in a spiral, to tie-in with Simon's carousel-type music. And he wanted the Thames ('... *somewhere in the East-end, where that bend in the river occurs ...'*) picked out in blue. In fact, he wanted the shape of the River Thames, an outline recognised all over the world, to be the logo for East 8 ... ('East 8?' Wasn't that only a working title? What was the actual title going to be? Don't think about it, things like programme titles have a habit of creeping up on you from behind when you least expected them, and usually they've been staring you in the face all the time!) There was a long way to go before Simon and Jeapes' opening and closing sequences would be completed, but at least everyone knew what they were aiming for.

Getting that infuriatingly catchy tune out of their heads was virtually impossible but they had to try, at least because there was still a lot of unfinished business to clear up, and it would require all their powers of concentration. Just a little thing like the writing of episodes one and two! Episodes three to six had been delivered, soon to be joined by more, as two other writing teams had been set in motion. As a definite 'house style' was starting to emerge, it was clearly the right time to commission the opening pair. But who, out of their growing list of writers, should be entrusted with such an important undertaking? Julia would have liked Tony to have started the serial off. He was, after all, one of the parents responsible for giving the baby life. But sheer pressure of work, all the storylining, commissioning, reading, rewriting and editing necessary to get the show off the ground at all, ruled that out of the question. They hit upon a solution. An answer that might in the end disappoint someone, but an answer that might give them a strong start. They would commission two authors, to write two different versions of the first sixty minutes. Jane Hollowood and Gerry Huxham were selected (probably because they were such opposites), briefed and sent away to their typewriters. Who knows? – perhaps the idea that they were competing might produce a little extra something out of the hat?

The sheer volume of technical considerations, and the constant plod of day-in, day-out logistic detail, forced the two of them to escape from the looking-glass world of Elstree and go back to the real East-end where it all began, before they too became just another pair of cogs in the infernal machine. They still needed a bank of people's names to draw on and clues as to how real East-end family life knitted together over the years. There was an instant resource available, cemeteries, where rows of headstones spoke the exit lines of generations. If the history of the East-end could be found anywhere it would surely be etched into those weather-worn stones, standing or lying sadly broken in overgrown wildernesses of graveyards.

Some inscriptions immediately spoke volumes, with the histories of entire families carved there by the stonemason's chisel.

'Died at Sea ... Died in the Great War ... Beloved Husband Of ... Died Aged Four Years ...'

Exotic names, Huguenot and Jewish were mixed in among the others, proof, if it was needed, of the successive waves of immigrants who had been swept up on the shores of the Thames. There was a 'Louisa Ada Beale'. There was a family named 'Copley' (the 'real' Pauline, Tony's cousin, was a Copley). They found a 'Victoria Amy Wicks' and an 'Albert George Luxford', who was born a year before the Battle of Trafalgar and died a hundred years later. They found the grave of General William Booth, founder of the Salvation Army. They made a note not to forget the Sally Army.

It was all there. Maybe they had found the last pieces of the jigsaw, those infernal pieces of blue sky that are always the hardest to fit in.

The last piece of jigsaw and the last days of June. One last thing still to do. If the East-end had been the inspiration for the idea, then that Shepherds Bush wine-bar had been where the words had begun. It was only proper that the words should end there too. Back they went, taking with them an A–Z of London. Their Square needed a name. Well, if it was built in the time of Queen Victoria, it ought to be named after her husband, Albert. Albert was also the name of Lou's husband, so there would be a constant reminder of the past. And, the pub should take the name of the Queen herself. 'Victoria and Albert' had a nice ring to it. The street connecting the square to the market would have to be 'Bridge Street' for obvious reasons. Which left the problem of what to call the road the market was in. During their early researches they had read that the East-end had once been the haunt of highwaymen, including the notorious Dick Turpin. His name gave rise to thoughts of villains and the underworld and so they chose 'Turpin Road'. For the Brewery, they opted for two of the names they had found at the cemetery, Luxford and Copley. And to keep going the reminders of the Second World War, the pub's bitter would be 'Churchill's'. ('*A pint of Churchill's, please!*') As to the name of the borough, Tony was keen for it to sound like Walthamstow, because of his family connections there. They looked through the A–Z at the maps of the real East-end, Stratford … Then on, into Essex … Ilford, Romford, Chelmsford. 'Ford' had an instant appeal. And by taking the first three letters of the place where the actual Beales and Fowlers came from, Walford was arrived at. The numbers of the East-end boroughs go in alphabetical order and start at 1 and end at 18. East 19 sounded clumsy. East 20 had a more rounded feeling to it.

And there it was! Albert Square, Walford, London, E.20. A world of their very own.

Much later, a journalist was prompted to write: '*It's like playing God in Shepherds Bush.*'

July, 1984. '*Have you got any actors yet?*'

'*Well, if it's London, East 20, you can't call it East 8, can you? So what **are** you going to call it?*'

'*I'm sorry – there's just not enough recording time. I must have facilities in the afternoon to record children and babies …*'

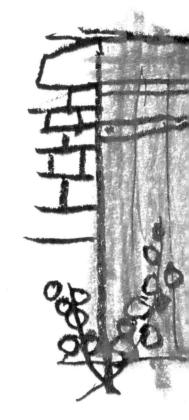

A corner of Albert Square.

'The reason we need that many dressing rooms is because the artists will be here at Elstree six days a week! It will be their second home, for heaven's sake!'

'I'm an assistant floor manager, Julia. I don't mind sorting out Elstree, getting rehearsal furniture and props and all that. But, cleaning the lavatories!'

'Caravans on the Lot? Fridges in the dressing rooms? This isn't Dallas, Julia!'

'Have you got any actors yet . . .?'

No, Julia hadn't got a single actor. But daily she was sending off letters to agents, fringe-theatres and drama schools. *'Dear Agent, here is a breakdown of the characters required for East 8. Only genuine East-enders need apply . . .'*

And in every letter she was careful not to give the whole game away, just snippets of the biographies, and never the complete list of characters. It only needed one or two smart agents gossiping over a glass of Muscadet, putting two and two together, and the whole concept of the show could be blown and appearing on 'Crossroads' before you could say Albion Market.

'Julia? It's Jonathan. Have you got any scripts I can look at yet?'

13 July, 1984. The Anna Scher Theatre is in North London. Anna is a pushy, vital Irish woman who takes her adrenalin neat. Unlike a lot of drama schools, where the students are admitted, ironed-out and then sent into the outside world as 'actors' all looking and sounding much like one another, Anna's school cashes in on what the students already have, themselves. She doesn't flatten their personalities or their natural accents even, on the contrary, she encourages them to bring them out and to use them. Her students aren't taught how to act, they're helped to dig inside themselves and *be*. Just the sort of non-acting acting that East 8 (or was it to be East 20?) was looking for.

Every so often the school has an 'open evening' – a showcase, if you like, when interested parties can go along and watch the students being put through their paces. Julia and Tony had been invited to attend just such an evening. They invariably start with a warm-up session that consists of a lot of hand-clapping and a sing-along, during which the audience is encouraged to partici-pate. Then the class is split into groups and various improvisations are staged based on a variety of given situations. The end results of these unstructured forays are often extremely funny, sometimes shockingly raw. Having used several of Anna's students in their previous productions, Julia and Tony were anxious to find out how the present intake would match up to them. Not all the participants in the classes are new, frequently, old students will drop by just to keep their hand in. On the night that Julia and Tony were there, Judith Jacob had decided to make an appearance. She was an old friend from 'Angels' days, when she'd been one of the 'regs'. And a young actress called Susan Tully was there too. Although still a teenager, she'd scored a considerable success for herself playing the character of Suzanne in 'Grange Hill'.

After one of these 'evenings', the audience is as drained as the performers, having been subjected in one night to a gamut of emotions wiser people would spread thinly over an entire lifetime. On the journey back to the Bush, the two of them considered the evening's fireworks. Judith Jacob had been as good as ever. But there wasn't really a part for her. Susan Tully had been very impressive. Natural and unaffected, she had displayed hidden depths of emotion inside herself. Perhaps they should meet her? Or was it a bad idea to cast someone whose face was already well known from another show? Wouldn't it suspend belief in the reality they were after?

There was a third person who had caught their attention. Gillian somebody-or-other (whatever the surname was, it was unpronounceable). She was a stunningly attractive blonde, slightly older than most of the others. But it wasn't her looks, or the range of her acting skills that had drawn them to her. It was her voice. Not the accent, either, which they guessed to be genuine Eastend. But, the voice itself, husky, adenoidal even – it seemed incongruously at odds with her appearance. She might make an interesting Sue, at the cafe. But then they'd never pictured Sue as a blonde. They'd seen her as dark. Kathy, perhaps? No, unfortunately, she was far too young to play Kathy. Never mind! She was certainly someone to bear in mind for the future.

The cast interviews began. They were to last three months. Already telephone lines were jammed from dawn till office-closing, with agents convinced that they could, singlehandedly, supply the entire cast, and actors and actresses who'd been told by so-and-so (who'd got it from whatsisname) that Julia Smith was casting! And, the morning mailbag was threatening to give the postman a permanent stoop. Out poured hundreds of letters and photographs. These were sorted into piles – male, female, east London, south London, north and west. (Letters from artists who were non-London were placed in a separate reject pile, and it took over eight months to send them all back!) Some actors, of course,

The first generation, the founding cast of EastEnders round the piano at the Queen Vic in a picture taken to commemorate the show's first Christmas, 1985: Wendy Richard, Anna Wing, Bill Treacher, Linda Davidson, Ross Davidson, Gretchen Franklin (with Willy the pug), Shirley Cheriton, Susan Tully, Leslie Grantham, Letitia Dean, Tom Watt, Anita Dobson, Leonard Fenton, Andrew Johnson, Paul J. Medford, John Altman, Oscar James, Roly, June Brown, Sandy Ratcliffe, Nejdet Salih, Gillian Taylforth, Adam Woodyatt, Nick Berry and Peter Dean.

The casting of EastEnders was no easy matter. Actors had not only to look the part but work together as convincing family groups. With the Fowlers it certainly seemed to work. **Centre**: Anna Wing as Lou Beale, **top left**: Wendy Richard as her

daughter Pauline, **top right**: Bill Treacher as her husband Arthur Fowler with **below left**: David Scarboro as their son Mark, a 'semi-regular' character, and **right**: Susan Tully as their daughter Michelle.

Best mates, Den Watts and Pete Beale
(centre), whose on-screen friendship
goes back to school days. Their families,
in spite of their own turbulent
relationships, have also made powerful on
screen friendships. **Top:** Gillian Taylforth
plays Kathy Beale. **Above:** Peter Dean
plays Pete Beale. **Right:** Adam Woodyatt
plays their son, Ian.

Top: Anita Dobson plays Angie Watts. Angie and Kathy Beale are also best friends. **Above:** Leslie Grantham plays Den Watts, the big fish in the small pond of Albert Square. **Left:** Letitia Dean plays Sharon, their adopted daughter.

Left: Sandy Ratcliff as Sue, the English wife of the Turkish–Cypriot cafe owner Ali Osman (above) played by Nejdet Salih. Haluk Bilginer plays his brother Mehmet.

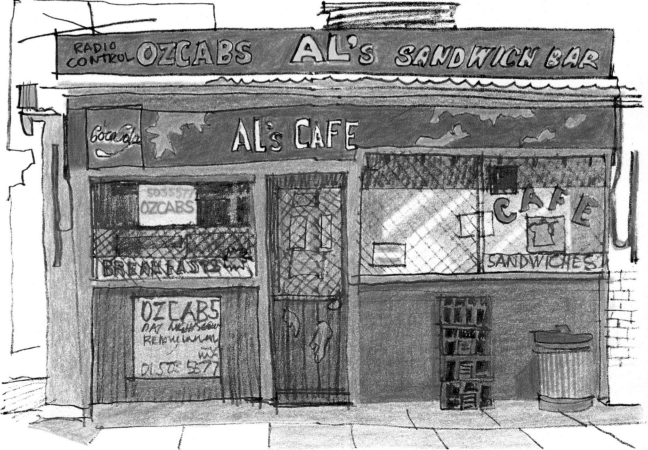

These characters represent a perception of a more traditional East-end with their memories of the Blitz and pre-war Docklands. **Left:** East End born Leonard Fenton plays Dr Harold Legg. **Above:** Gretchen Franklin as Ethel Skinner who 'does' for the Doctor. **Top:** June Brown as Dot, the arch-gossip of the Launderette and a character who bridges the generations.

Albert Square has its 'loners', characters who don't fit in to traditional family patterns. **Left:** Tom Watt as Lofty, the misfit who nevertheless cared enough to marry Michelle. **Below:** Out of make-up, Linda Davidson is hard to recognise as Mary, the rebel who struggles to bring up her baby alone in Albert Square.

Below: Michael Cashman plays Colin, the single professional man who was not to remain single for long.

Above: Shreela Ghosh plays Naima Jeffery, a character caught between two cultures, now on her own after her marriage to Saeed ended in divorce.

The new EastEnders. The characters of Debbie Wilkins (top left played by Shirley Cheriton) and Andy O'Brien (right played by Ross Davidson) were created to represent a young couple with upwardly mobile pretensions. But the formula did not work and both characters were eventually written out. However the arrival of Barbour-wearing James Willmott-Brown (above, played by William Boyd) to run the Dagmar allowed Julia and Tony to explore the impact of the Yuppy invasion on the East-end in a much more robust manner.

A Deco wall light

marble wallpaper

Blue

Midg

INTerior DAGMAR

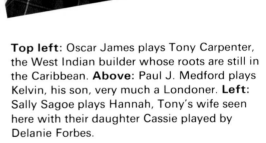

Top left: Oscar James plays Tony Carpenter, the West Indian builder whose roots are still in the Caribbean. **Above**: Paul J. Medford plays Kelvin, his son, very much a Londoner. **Left**: Sally Sagoe plays Hannah, Tony's wife seen here with their daughter Cassie played by Delanie Forbes.

Right: 'The Banned' the Albert Square rock group that featured most of the show's younger cast members. Recordings by Nick Berry and by Letitia Dean with Paul J. Medford actually got into the charts ('Every Loser Wins' was at number one for three weeks). But off-screen success meant storyline problems.

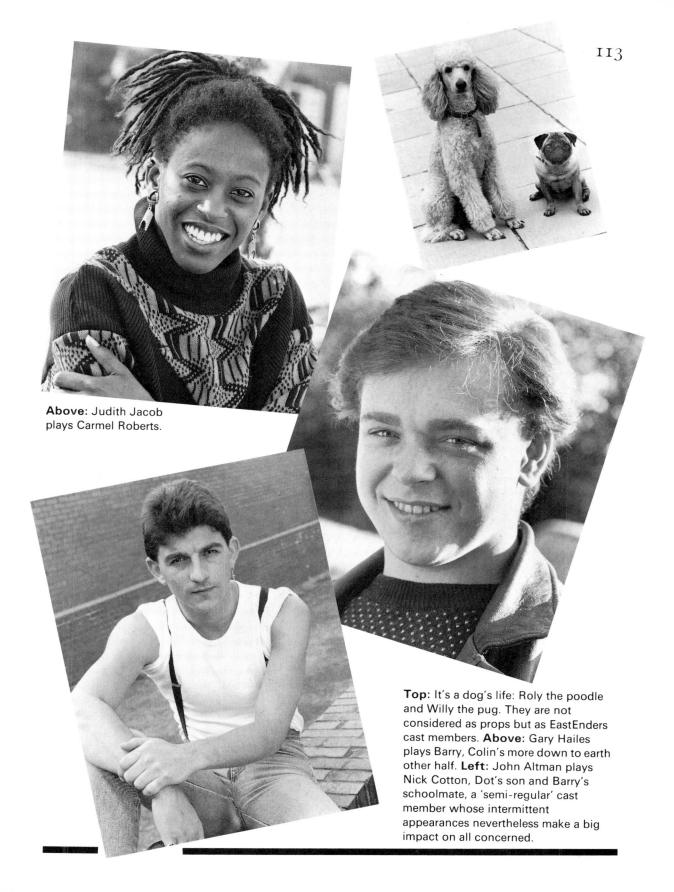

Above: Judith Jacob
plays Carmel Roberts.

Top: It's a dog's life: Roly the poodle
and Willy the pug. They are not
considered as props but as EastEnders
cast members. **Above:** Gary Hailes
plays Barry, Colin's more down to earth
other half. **Left:** John Altman plays
Nick Cotton, Dot's son and Barry's
schoolmate, a 'semi-regular' cast
member whose intermittent
appearances nevertheless make a big
impact on all concerned.

From unknowns to stars – two years on from that cast shot in the Queen Vic and the EastEnders look as if they have all the confidence that success brings. It's an interesting exercise to spot the entrances and exits in two turbulent years – new arrivals include William Boyd as James Willmott-Brown, Katherine Apanowicz as Mags, Michael Cashman as Colin, Donald Tandy as Tom, Judith Jacob as Carmel, Pam St Clements as Pat Wicks, and Garry Hailes as Barry.

didn't need to send letters and photos asking if they could be in East 20. In some cases, Julia and Tony asked to see *them*.

When Bill Treacher walked through the office door, he didn't exactly look like an 'Arthur'. For a start, his well-pressed suit had not been picked up at a jumble sale, and his hair was far too well cut. His warm, open face was smiling, as if he didn't have a trouble in the world. He was also clearly well fed! All the things that Arthur was not. Yet, if he had wanted the part, he could have had it there and then, because he'd been the first actor they had thought of for the show, in fact, Arthur had almost been invented with him in mind. He was no stranger to Julia and Tony. Tony had first met him in the days, years before, when he had also been an actor, and they'd been in 'Rep' together. And they had both worked with him on 'Z Cars'. His qualities as an actor were exactly the ones they wanted for the very difficult part of Arthur. Warmth, directness and an ability to be convincingly ordinary without being dull.

As they were to do on countless occasions with different artists over the coming weeks, they explained a little about the show and a good deal more about the character that they had Bill in mind for, being careful to point out that, for the first two years at least, Arthur would be a very depressing man to portray. At the end of the interview, Bill seemed highly chuffed. He was definitely interested, and, at the moment anyway, had no commitments that he knew of for when rehearsals were due to begin. But there was to be no immediate offer. He had to do a lot of hard thinking, the sort of high-profile exposure he could possibly get as one of the stars of a popular soap opera, might drastically alter his life. Added to which, the working schedule promised to be punishing and relentless. Bill and his family lived in the country. Just how prepared was he to commit himself to a job that could cause major upheavals in his home life?

The 'Angels' audience had fallen in a big way for Shirley Cheriton, the actress who played 'Katy'. She'd been a real glamour-girl in the 'Miss World' sense and received sackfuls of fan mail. As she had progressed, series after series, from student nurse to staff nurse, so her acting skills had grown with her. Each year, as she was called on to do more, and give more, she'd risen to the challenge with reserves to spare. She'd also been a good 'company' member to have around – sensible and practical. Perhaps she seemed more conventional than the other 'Angels'. Happily married, head screwed on right and her feet on the ground. Was she now ready to tackle the part of 'Debbie', the bossy interfering lady from the bank? She would be one of the 'outsiders' of Albert Square, and not necessarily the most sympathetic character in the show, either. Shirley was herself a rung or two up from her working-class origins, as the part was meant to be, but she wasn't posh, and could never be mistaken for a trendy or a Sloane. At the interview, Tony and Julia noticed that she had lost weight since 'Angels', the puppy-fat had vanished. She was sleeker, more elegant, and had grown up a lot. She liked the sound of 'Debbie Wilkins'. It would be something new for her, to play a person who wasn't immediately liked by everyone. Since they'd last seen her, she'd had a baby. Would that cause problems? None at all! There was no conflict between the family-lady and the career-lady in her life, she'd got it all organised. As usual, Shirley was the professional down to her fingertips. (Married to a policeman in real life, Tony and Julia had married Shirley's character in 'Angels' to a policeman, played by Gary Whelan. Although no-one could know it at the time, Shirley – as 'Debs' – was destined to marry another policeman in EastEnders, also played by Gary Whelan!)

Sandy Ratcliffe had been Snowdon's 'Face of the Sixties'. And she must possess one of the most photogenic faces on television. She had been recommended for the part of Sue by writer Bill Lyons. (She had been in several of Bill's plays for 'Schools'.) There was a toughness in her face and manner, a fiery gypsy-like quality. And she sounded East-end enough. Sue had to be hard, and clearly Sandy would be able to do that standing on her head, but Sue was also a loser, and a victim. On the surface, Sandy appeared to be the reverse. A staunch feminist, she wanted to know why we couldn't make the cafe into a Women's-only bookshop. Would her own personality and strongly held views be at odds with the character? As an actress, playing a 'part' and not herself, did it matter? But as a 'political' actress, would Sandy put up with it? And how would she react to the strict disciplines of twice-weekly drama, where every second counts? She was not renowned for being the most disciplined person in the world, more the free spirit. Anyway, she couldn't be cast until they'd found her husband, Ali. And *where* were they going to find a Turkish-Cypriot actor . . .?!

At the end of the first casting interviews there was a possibility that they had found three of the twenty-three. But, just as Sue was dependent on who played Ali so Arthur was dependent on who was cast as Pauline, and she was dependent on who played her twin brother, Pete. Just as Debs had to be 'right' with Andy. And where in London were there two Bengali-speaking artists?

When the casting sessions began, the first twenty-two scripts had been commissioned and were either being written, rewritten or edited. Writers' meetings were now taking place on a regular basis and the mountains of work had convinced the powers-that-be that the script-editor should have an assistant, who could double as researcher. Tony had managed to find a black, East-end writer. *('I suppose you want me to write for the programme because of the black characters?' 'No . . . what are you like with Jews?')* But his list of genuine East-end literary talent was still slim.

'Dear Agent, Do you represent any writers who are genuine East-enders . . .?'

As a result of letters, photos, agents' recommendations and word of mouth, a shortlist of artists to be seen was drawn up. The weeding-out process, involving by now several hundred actors, had taken ages, and left approximately four possibles for every part, nearly every part that is. The shortlist was a bit flimsy when it came to Bengalis, Turkish-Cypriots and West Indians.

Working together for as long as they had, the duo had developed certain sly techniques when it came to interviewing people. They occupied separate but adjoining offices with a communicating door. During interviews, Julia with artists and Tony with writers, the door was kept shut. If one of them felt the person they were seeing had something to offer, then the door was casually thrown open. This was a sign to the other to 'wander in . . . as if you just wanted to pass the time of day . . . and see if you agree that I've found someone of interest . . .' Tony had written audition scenes for every character (and every combination of characters) and one-by-one the actors were wheeled in to see the boss-lady. Many times over the next few weeks the door connecting Julia's office to Tony's was to be 'casually thrown open . . .'

'Tony, I'd like you to meet Anna Wing . . .'

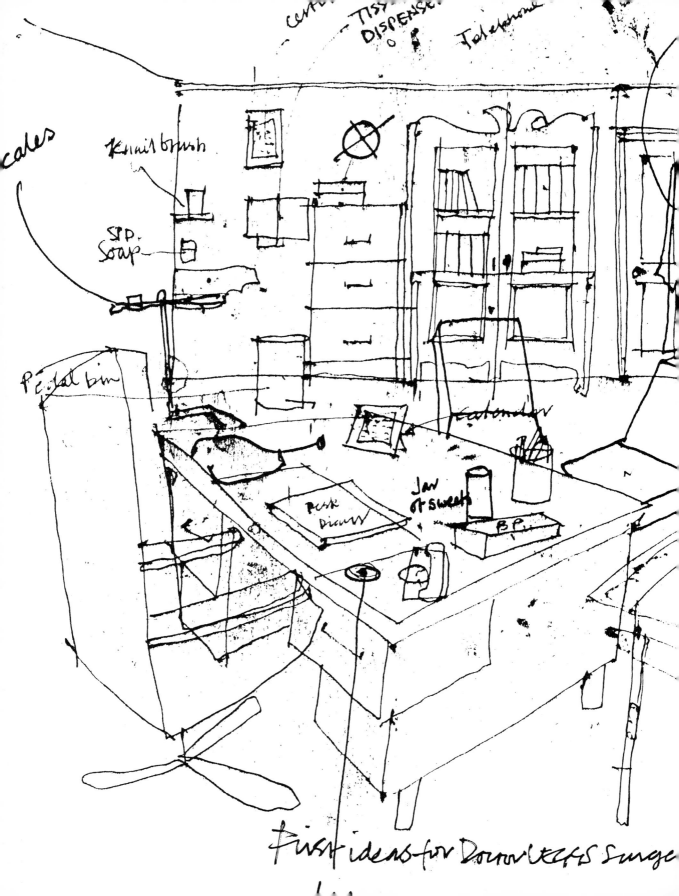

cales

Knail brush

STP.
Soap

Pedal bin

TISSUE
DISPENSE

Telephone

Calendar

Jar
of sweets

Desk
Diary

B.P.

First ideas for Doctor Keffs Surge

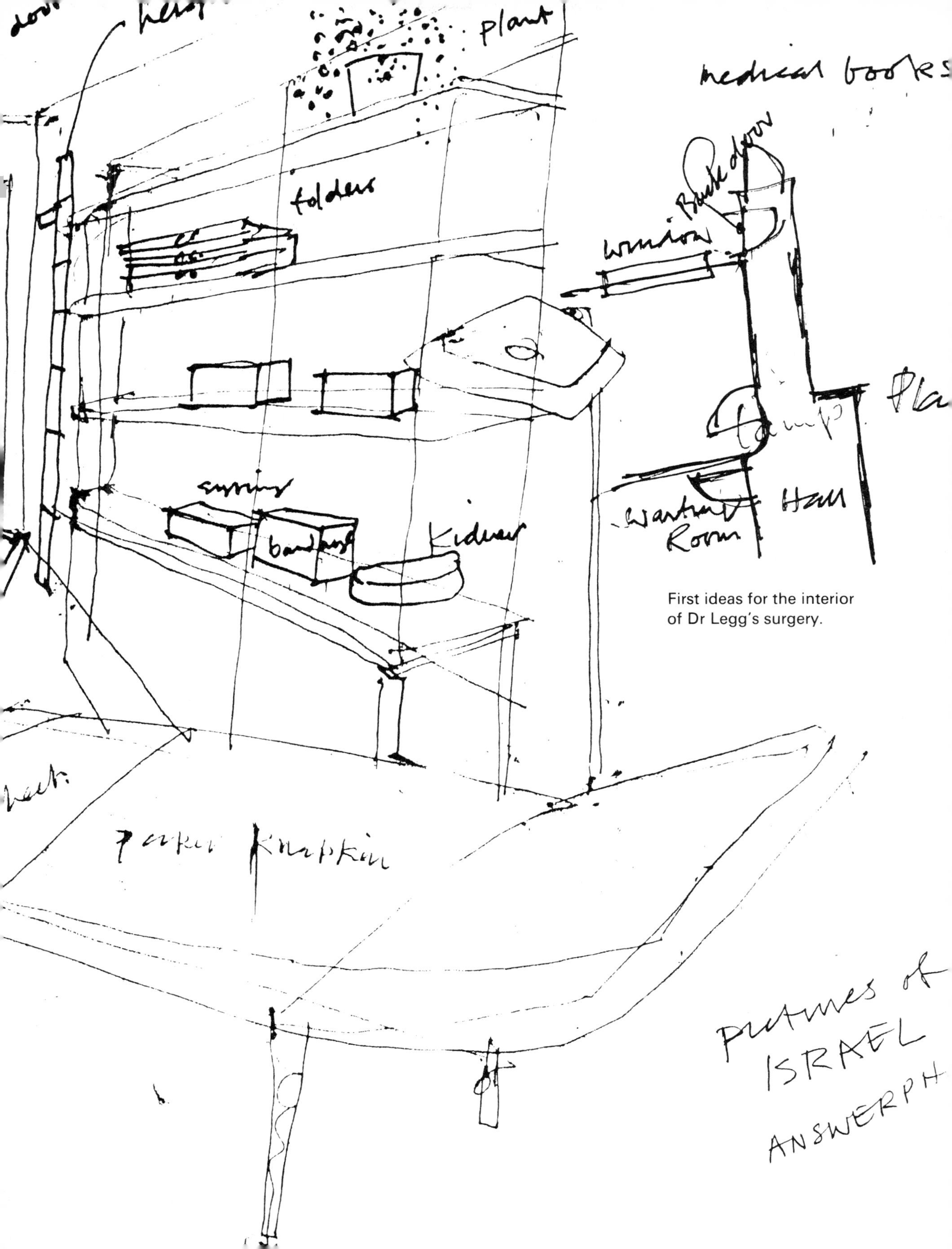

door
shelf
plant
medical books
folders
window
Bookshelf
lamp
Pla
Waiting Room
Hall
curtain
bandage
Kidney
shelf
paper Knapkin
pictures of
ISRAEL
ANSWERPH

First ideas for the interior
of Dr Legg's surgery.

Anna, up for the part of Lou, matriarch and backbone of the programme, was all ear-rings, sepia photographs of her grand-parents in the East-end (Anna was born in Hackney), wonderful tales of her childhood, and sweet naughtiness, intended to shock. When she first read for the part, she overacted terribly, but on the second reading (less nervous) brought the performance down considerably. She was almost the right age for Lou, but there were tough questions to consider, such as would she have the stamina to survive the schedule? And what was her memory like for learning lines – every week? When asked if she'd like to be in a popular soap, she replied, *'All my life I've been an actress, now I want to be a household name!'*

There was however the small problem of an offer of a part in the 'Adrian Mole' play, and the dates would clash with 'Walford, E.20' (or was it to be just: 'Walford'?). Julia, never one to give in to blackmail, threw the ball straight back into Anna's court. The actress would have to take a gamble. She could either turn down the play offer, which would mean if she didn't get the part of Lou she'd have lost two jobs. Or she could wave goodbye to any possibility of ever playing Lou, and accept the part in the play. At least that way she'd have one job to go to. It was up to her . . . Hot on the heels of the interview a phone-call arrived for Julia from Anna's agent. Anna had turned down the part in the 'Adrian Mole' play.

'This is Tom Watt. One of our writers suggested him for Lofty . . .'

The invention of Lofty (George) Holloway had been an after-thought, and he was still something of an enigma to his creators and writers alike. Julia and Tony hadn't a clue what they were looking for and kidded themselves that when a 'Lofty' walked through that door, they would know it. And Tom Watt had walked through the door. He was tall, pale and skinny. He looked physically gauche, vulnerably childlike and accident-prone – like a Frank Spencer in spectacles. The spectacles seemed an integral part of his face, you could imagine him being born wearing them. After the glasses, you noticed his hair, which was short, spiky and clearly had a life of its own. He was certainly different . . .

'Leonard Fenton, may I introduce the script-editor?'

They were anticipating problems with the casting of Doctor Legg. Actors of the right age, intelligence and class, who could play Jewish professional men, were difficult to track down. They'd either left the business, or were too closely identified with other programmes. Leonard Fenton was another suggestion of Bill Lyons. (*'If you want the best, it's got to be Leonard.'*) Leonard understood the character at once, though he questioned the accuracy of the surname: Legg. He was fascinated by the Doctor's passionate concern for the community and his great love of music, something that Leonard and Legg had in common. He seemed

Above: Anna Wing embraced the part of Lou Beale, and the prospect of becoming a household name, with gleeful enthusiasm. Leonard Fenton identified with the part of Dr Legg straightaway from his own childhood in Stepney.

perfect for the part. But he was already signed-up to appear in a new series of 'Shine on, Harvey Moon', and the recording dates overlapped. Julia wondered if she should call the producer of his other show, and see if they might work out a 'deal'.

Subject to hassles with her agent (did she really approve of her artists appearing in soaps?) it looked as if Sandy Ratcliffe was hot favourite for the part of Sue. But casting her husband, Ali, remained a problem. In the whole of London only three Turkish-speaking actors could be located, and one of them was completely wrong for the part. The other two, though, were possibles. Haluk Bilginer was Turkish and almost type-casting for the 'pea-cock' they were looking for, right down to Bandito moustache and hairy chest! Nejdet Salih was Turkish-Cypriot and had a background surprisingly similar to Ali's. Although needing con-siderable persuasion to indicate the swaggering physicality of the macho-man (perhaps they had been too long in England) they read well and were both in with a chance. So, not having to worry about their acting potential, other aspects could be considered.

Here, Julia and Tony had another of their famous fights. Tony favoured Haluk for the part, so that they got the 'look' of the man right. In his opinion, Nejdet simply was not tall or tough-looking enough. He didn't have the sort of physical presence that put you on your guard, he was more like a teddy-bear asking for a cuddle. Sandy Ratcliffe would have made mincemeat of him. Furthermore, there was no way that he was going to be able to grow a moustache! (A point Tony was to be proved right on!) Julia disagreed. Nejdet was the genuine article. Not Turkish, but Turkish-Cypriot. He would have so much actual knowledge to bring to the character. He lived in the East-end, as did his large family. He wouldn't have to act the part, he *was* the part. The only way to try and resolve the dilemma was to bring the two actors back for a second reading, this time with the actress who would probably end up playing the wife to one or other of them. Both actors arrived on time for this meeting. The actress didn't. Nejdet and Haluk had to be kept waiting, in separate rooms, until Sandy made her entrance (and excuses) forty-five minutes later.

Haluk read first. He had obviously thought about the part since the first interview because there was much more physical power in his performance. At one stage Julia and Tony were worried that he might even hit Sandy! Nejdet was second to read. He was introduced to Sandy and given lots of apologies for having been kept waiting so long for her arrival. He winked at Julia and Tony, and said: *'Not to worry. Typical bloody woman!'* He almost got the part on the strength of that one line alone. For a split second they could see Ali!

The irony was that they would both get a part. There were only two suitable Turkish-speaking actors in London, and Ali would need a brother.

'This is Peter Dean . . .'

Tony recognised him from the gritty BBC crime drama 'Law and Order'. He looked uncannily like the person he was based on, and was surely absolutely perfect for 'Pete Beale'? He was from the East-end of London and his family was still working a stall in the market. (This was almost too good to be true! It meant that he would probably know the right way to do things. What you did and what you didn't do on a market stall.) He had so much chat at the interview and such a fund of stories that he was in danger of turning into a 'professional cockney' on the spot. His tremendous enthusiasm for the part and the show made up for the disappointing reading he gave. Maybe it was 'nerves'? Maybe it was something else? Up to this point his acting career had been conducted mainly on film, that is shot by shot, line by line. A big question therefore was how would he stand up to multi-camera work, where whole scenes were recorded at a time?

'Letitia Dean. No relation to Peter . . .'

On the strength of a photograph, Letitia was being seen for the part of Sharon, Den's 'princess', and his adopted daughter. The character was meant to be fourteen, but – because of licensing regulations – would have to be played by a sixteen-year-old, who could 'play down'. What they were looking for was a bouncy, attractive, oddly vulnerable young woman who would come across as slightly more sophisticated than Michelle. Of all the actresses they'd seen up to now, only Letitia had all those things. She also had something else, that was to prove the clincher, the dirtiest laugh in the world!

*'Julia? it's Jonathan: No sign of a **title** yet?'*

'We're working on it . . .'

'Any chance I could look at some scripts . . .?'

Two versions of episodes one and two had been delivered that day. Normally Julia and Tony leap onto scripts at the first available moment, but this time they held back, knowing how important these particular bundles of paper were to the initial impact of the programme. But their uncharacteristic restraint concealed other considerations. What if Jane's pair were better than Gerry's? Or Gerry's better than Jane's? How would one of them react to having their episodes 'pulled'? And how would Tony summon up the courage to tell the unlucky person? Or worse, supposing neither set came up to scratch?

The final outcome couldn't have been more satisfactory, both versions, with the minimum of alterations, were excellent. But, Gerry's opening episode just had the edge on Jane's, and Jane's second episode was marginally punchier than Gerry's. Episodes one and two of 'Walford' with two different authors were ready!

'You must know Gretchen Franklin . . .?'

Everyone in the business did. She had been the first name to come into everyone's heads whenever 'Ethel' was mentioned, Ethel, with her 'little Willy' never far away, close friend to Lou and Lofty. Gretchen had been in the business since the year dot, and would be a marvellous 'old-pro' to have in the company. At the reading she went way over the top.

'Bring it down a bit, Gretchen. Bring it down. You're not at the London Palladium!'

She did bring it down. Just . . . Gretchen was ideal casting. But how would she manage the journeying to Elstree and back six days a week? And, would an actress of her standing agree to appear in a soap, anyway?

By the end of July half the characters of 'Walford' (or should it be 'London, Walford, E.20' or should it be 'Albert Square') had names pencilled in beside them. Julia was running out of artists

Left: Peter Dean actually comes from a stall-holding London family and his casting as Pete Beale was particularly fortuitous. In contrast more people were seen for the part of Kathy Beale than for any other character. Gillian Taylforth was really too young for the role (Kathy would have a teenage son) but her freshness and earthy charm finally won her the part.

EPISODES 1 - 31

DEN, ANGIE, SHARON

Den, Arthur and Ali find Reg Cox's body.

The Area Manager catches Den carrying in a case of whiskey. To cover himself, Den says it's for a private party and invites the Area Manager. At the party, the Area Manager fails to turn up, but Angie makes a pass at Lofty.

Den wants to make alterations to the pub. His proposals are being considered by the brewery. Angie would prefer to move away.

Den's mistress, Jane, wants the two of them to go away on holiday to Spain together. Angie gets suspicious. He spins a yarn to Angie, buys her a microwave and takes her out to dinner. She's still suspicious. He telephones from Spain with his number and Angie calls back and gets to speak to Jane. Den calls back with a cock 'n bull story about how Jane was the caretaker. He's got to stay another week. Meanwhile Angie starts a flirtation with Tony which grows into a full-scale love affair. Sharon suspects this and blackmails Angie who has to tell Sharon about Den and Jane. Once Den returns, there are dramas all round. Angie admits she's been having an affair as well, though she won't name Tony. Den and Angie decide to patch it up for Sharon's sake. They get it together for the first time in fifteen years. Den goes off to finish with Jane. Tony gives Angie a bracelet which she has to give to Sharon to avoid suspicion from Den. Tony sees Sharon wearing it and, naturally, is upset. Den's beginning to suspect Tony anyway. Sharon and Michelle are rivals for Kelvin. Sharon gets herself a date with him but he tells her to cool it. Once Kelvin and Michelle get into a steady relationship, Sharon feels threatened. She tells Kelvin she'll go further than Michelle and consults Dr Legg about going on the Pill.

THE FAMILY - LOU, ARTHUR, PAULINE, MICHELLE, MARK

Arthur, together with Den and Ali, finds Reg Cox's body.

Pauline's pregnant; Lou's furious. Various unsuccessful attempts are made to pacify her including a special Sunday dinner until finally she's packed off to Clacton for a holiday with a reluctant Michelle as companion.

Both Arthur and Mark are suspects for Reg's murder. The Fowlers themselves are suspicious of Mark, particularly when they're also summoned to his school. It turns out he's been using his school dinner money to buy fags. He gets very friendly with Nick and becomes a skinhead. He's lectured about associating with Nick and when Nick's caught it's likely he'll be called as a witness. He goes onto a YTS scheme, dislikes it, gets the sack. Lou tells Ian about Pete in his young days and Ian confides that he feels caught between his parents. Lou rows with Pete and Kathy over Ian.

Arthur gets a temporary job at the pub and another one working for Tony. He covers for Den when he's away. Michelle and Sharon keep making anonymous telephone calls to Ali in order to bait Sue. Once Sue and Ali discover, the two girls are in trouble. They are also rivals for Kelvin. Michelle wants to invite him home but Mark's against it. When Michelle returns from Clacton she's full of an alleged romance with a waiter called Chas. The others are determined to catch Michelle out.

These are abbreviated story lines from the first months of the show, used to brief writers who joined the team later. Den's mistress, referred to as 'Jane' was changed to 'Jan' as Leslie Grantham's real-life wife is called Jane.

- 2 -

Mark and Ian call the pub and leave a message that Chas called. Michelle guesses and plays along. She invites him to see the video Mark has got hold of and is planning to charge the others to watch. They have to rope in a puny friend of Mark's to pretend to be Chas. Pete and Kathy interrupt them all watching the video which turns out to be a porno movie, turf them out and settle down to watch it themselves.

Lou's been complaining of feeling ill. It's diagnosed as shingles. Coping with it causes tension in the Fowler household. Arthur is made to feel guilty about being unemployed but isn't allowed to help with Lou who takes the wrong drugs and hallucinates. Pauline feels more and more hassled until she finally collapses and is taken to hospital suffering from exhaustion. Arthur begins to assert himself which causes conflict with Lou.

Michelle and Kelvin start a serious relationship. They go on a date together and are late back, causing havoc.

NICK

Nick is Reg Cox's murderer. He quarrels with Ali and is barred from the pub. He's the burglar on the estate and sells a stolen tool-box to Kelvin when Tony refuses it. He breaks into the foodstore. He gets himself invited to Ethel's flat and threatens her. He goes missing. It emerges he's a heroin addict and the murderer. He's charged and remanded in custody.

PETE, KATHY, IAN

Pete and Kathy are in on pacifying Lou, the Golden Circle story which is started by Sue, and Den and Angie's marital problems.

When Pete pushes Ian to be a 'man's man', Pete and Kathy argue over it and end up not talking until Pete refuses to open his stall until they make up, which they do. Then Kathy pressurises Ian to do well at school. Again Pete and Kathy row. Ian blows, confides in Lou, who interferes.

Angie approaches Ian to take over the catering in the pub once Ethel's efforts there are obviously a failure. Ian does it very well but nobody buys the food so he has to stop.

Pete and Kathy are opposed to the Council's rumoured plans to rebuild part of the Square.

It's Kathy's birthday the night the teenagers show the porno movie at the flat and Pete and Kathy interrupt them and settle down to watch it themselves.

SUE AND ALI

Ali's with Den and Arthur when they discover Reg Cox. He has a punch-up with Nick and is barred from the pub. He and Nick make it up and Ali's allowed back into the pub but when his minicab takings are stolen he suspects Nick and eventually confronts him.

as fast as Tony was gobbling-up writers. And the name of the show, they still did not have a name.

'Dear Agent, Here's a breakdown of the characters in the BBC's new bi-weekly. Only genuine East-enders need apply . . .'

'Dear Agent, Do you by any chance represent any writers who are genuine East-enders . . .?'

The communicating door flew open. Julia for all the world might have shouted 'Eureka!' The title had been staring them in the face all the time. They'd both used it in letters at least twice a day . . . East-enders. 'East-enders.' 'EAST-ENDERS'!

August, 1984. *'Julia? It's Jonathan. Are there any scripts ready yet?'*

'They're being typed. Be with you any day now . . .'

Paul J. Medford was becoming a fixation, as four separate agencies had sent in his picture and details. He was London born and bred and had been a child actor. Good-looking, fashionable and very street-cred he'd make a good Kelvin, if someone could be found to play his dad.

Several young actors were seen and read for the part of Mark, Pauline and Arthur's son. (Including Gary Hailes, who was later to play 'Barry'.) On paper, David Scarboro was the least likely to get the job. You couldn't see much of his face as most of it was obscured by a huge greased quiff that loomed dangerously down over his forehead and threatened to lop-off the end of his nose. You could see even less of it when he read, because he mumbled into his chest, as if he only wanted his leather jacket to hear the words. His eyes were piercing though, and there was a quality of James Dean about him – the duo reckoned he'd be dynamite on screen. And possibly pretty explosive off, too. He was so like Mark. And complete type-casting could be dangerous.

More people were seen for the part of Kathy Beale than for any other character. Each actress possessed some of the facets of personality wanted but not a single one had them all. Kathy had to be attractive, warm, practical, tough, funny and sexy! Gillian somebody-or-other came through the door, the person with the 'voice' that Julia and Tony had been so impressed with 'at Anna Scher's 'open-night'. As she came into the room, bringing the whole of the 'East-end' in with her, she was still grinning from a joke she'd been told in the corridor outside by a mate. (Susan Tully?) In exactly half a minute she'd charmed the pants off them. But, she was too young! They had said so from the beginning. By rights, they should not even be interviewing her. But wasn't she perfect, apart from her age? So different from any other 'Kathy' they had seen. Fresher. More down to earth. Ages were discussed, and a pocket-calculator produced. If Pete Beale had been her first boyfriend, wasn't it just possible that she could have a fourteen-year-old son? Julia and Tony were trying to talk themselves into it.

Gillian left, and was replaced by Susan Tully, another private joke being exchanged as their paths crossed. Susan was a known quantity so there was no need for her to 'sell' herself. The character of Michelle Fowler was outlined to her, including the story about her becoming a pregnant schoolgirl. *'Is she going to have the baby?'* Susan asked. When she was informed that she was, she added, *'Good!'* Susan explained that although she liked the part she'd played in 'Grange Hill', because the programme was set in a school, she'd never been allowed to grow up. The thing that excited her most about East-enders was that she'd be able to develop over a long period of time, and become an adult. Julia's initial worry about Susan playing Michelle was that her face was too well known. Could that fact be turned to the programme's advantage? She'd had a huge following on 'Grange Hill'. Would those fans now switch-on to East-enders, too?

'I believe you two know each other?'

Matthew Robinson, the lead-director, had brought Wendy Richard in to see Julia. Julia and Wendy hadn't worked together since 'The Newcomers'. There were hugs and kisses all round, and Matthew returned discreetly to his own office. Julia had thought of Wendy for the part of Pauline, but had made no approaches for three reasons. Firstly, the policy of the programme was not to use 'stars' and Wendy was already a household name. Secondly, the part of Pauline was not the most glamorous one in the world, and Wendy's current role in 'Are You Being Served?' was. And thirdly, Julia was frankly nervous that Wendy would say no! So, Matthew had seen her instead. Faced with Wendy, in the flesh, Julia wondered if her three reasons had been that important. Casually, Julia threw open the communicating door, Tony was introduced to Wendy, and they were left on their own. Wendy plonked herself down on a chair, and said, *'Thank God! Someone who smokes.'* She lit up and puffed away at a long cigarette holder. This, coupled with the dark glasses made her look like a 'forties movie-queen. Tony broached the subject of glamour. *'I'm sick of glamour,'* she said, exhaling cigarette smoke, *'I want to play my age. It's about time.'* She'd already been in several long running shows, and Tony wondered if she could face the thought of another one. *'I want to work, darling,'* she said. Matthew and Julia had already told her everything about the programme and she thought it sounded like a winner. Her actual words were: *'It sounds like the bollocks ....!'* They've been mates ever since.

Julia had her first meeting with the make-up supervisor. (*'We don't need make-up. Leave them as they are. Just a slight difference between the way they look at work, or school, and the way they look when they're at play ... And we don't pay for tints. If we book 'em blonde, they* **stay** *blonde!'*) And the costume designer. (*'Nothing to "design" – why are you given such grand titles? Makes you want to go out and do things to justify it ... Lots of London colours. Grey – and subdued ...'*)

And a little game called 'Happy Families' began ...

More audition scenes were written and artists who were being considered for the various parts were called back. This time they were put together in family groups. This was going to be a very important test – could you believe in them as families? Was the hair-colouring right? The heights? The variety in the voices? Were the actors getting on? Did Pauline and Arthur look as if they'd been married for however long it was? Did Kathy look old enough to have that son? Could you imagine Mark and Ian as cousins? Did Lou look like the mother of Pauline and Pete? And could Pauline and Pete pass for twins? It was a lengthy session, that took place in several offices at once. At the end of it everyone went home after being told that their agents would get a phone call.

Wendy Richard was a familiar face from several long running TV shows, an actress with a great talent for comedy. Although the policy of the show was not to use established stars, casting her as Pauline Fowler, not a particulary glamorous role, was a leap of faith which landed smack on its feet.

Julia and Tony were left alone. It had to be admitted, they did work as a family. They looked like one, sounded like one and felt like one. All except little Ian. He wasn't quite right. Slipped up there. But the dream was coming true, the chemistry was working, Julia and Tony had got their big East-end family! Apart from Ian . . .

While an advertisement went into *The Stage* newspaper asking for Bengali-speaking actors in their early twenties, Julia returned to the search for Tony Carpenter, Kelvin's dad. She asked herself what black actors could she remember using on 'Angels'? – there must have been dozens. But some of those approached were either already in work, or 'didn't do soaps . . .' (There's a premium on good black actors, and they can afford to be fussy.) Then Oscar James' face was suddenly staring up at her from the pages of *Spotlight*, the actors' casting directory. Oscar had a tremendous amount of experience in telly, theatre and films, and he had not been seen on the box too much recently. He was worth a thought . . .

Oscar was physically a much bigger man than they'd originally had in mind. His interpretation of Tony would be expansive and get noticed. It was also a nice idea for father and son to be not only different ages, but different physical types as well. Storywise, it might be possible to build on this and also give them different attitudes. At the meeting with Oscar, he was full of praise for the way the team had chosen to depict a black family. It was a bit throwing for Julia and Tony as they had not really thought of Tony and Kelvin as being particularly black. Their story is really meant to be about a developing relationship between a father and a son. More 'Happy Families . . .' Oscar and Paul read together, and Oscar started giving 'notes' to Paul about how they ought to play the scene. Already he was starting to take him under his wing, just like a father . . .

'Leslie Grantham? Never heard of him . . .'

'Wait a minute. Didn't I use to teach him at drama school?'

Matthew had tossed the name into the meeting. It meant nothing to the other director present, but rang a bell with Julia. She'd remembered teaching someone with that name at The

Webber-Douglas Drama School. She couldn't recall much about his appearance – but had a recollection that he'd been a 'mature student'. Well at least she knew he'd been well trained, if nothing else! Trouble was, she had never seen him in action. He came into the office. Just about everything he said was a 'gag' but, when you looked at his white knuckles and the sweat on his forehead, you realised that this was just a device to cover extreme nervousness. Despite his nerves, he read very well. Julia and Tony studied him. Den had to be an unknown. Well, he scored full marks in that department. He had to be 'starry'. They'd reserve judgment on that one. But he couldn't be so 'starry' that he would not accept BBC fees. No problem there either. But also, Den had to have panache, charisma, electricity.

Mr Grantham certainly had something, a good sense of humour for starters. But, more than that, tensed up internal emotion of some sort that was only just being held in. There was something behind the eyes, too. Barely contained violence almost . . . Better think about this one. Anyway, no firm offers could even be considered until they'd come up with an Angie. Couldn't possibly cast a Den without an Angie . . .

When Leslie Grantham had gone, neither of them was sure. There were the makings of a 'Den' certainly – but was there enough? Julia thought he might have 'sex appeal'. Tony reckoned he was too slim – publicans ought to be big.

'Julia? It's Jonathan. I'm not happy with this title.'

'Let's talk some time . . .'

' When do I see the scripts?'

'This afternoon.'

Unable to stall any longer, Tony and Julia sent the first six episodes of East-enders off to their Head of Department. It was now or never . . .

So, Jonathan wasn't sure about the title? Well, neither were they. They knew it was the right word, but couldn't decide how it should look. Should it be one word, or should it be two? Should it be in small letters, or in capital letters? Alan Jeapes made up some designs for them to look at. 'EAST ENDERS' and 'East Enders'. And 'EASTENDERS' and 'Eastenders'. After staring at the letters for hours, they were starting to see double. None of the versions looked right, but something was bound to turn up . . .

'I don't like your title, Tony. It's difficult to say and so ugly!'

'Have you found an Ian yet . . .?'

It had happened that husband and wife characters in a popular TV soap in India, played by a couple who were also married in real life, had to divorce each other on screen. When the scene was completed, they considered themselves actually divorced and had to re-marry. The Muslim faith is not just a religion, after all, it's a way of life. Was this why there were so few Bengali-speaking actresses in London? Was it against their religious beliefs to go on 'public display'? Could the answer be as simple as that?

A sprinkling of replies to the various advertisements and enquiries landed on Julia's desk. One from a model, and she was the wrong age. Another from an interviewer, and she would never be able to master the difficult job of acting. One good actress was known, and she was almost offered the part of Naima on the spot, but she 'wouldn't do soaps . . .'

Shreela Ghosh was a late arrival. A very intelligent woman, she understood and liked what they were trying to do with the young Asian couple. She was comparatively inexperienced, but she was the perfect age and looked right. Andrew Johnson, up for the part of Saeed, had a lot in common with the character. Like Saeed, he'd been born of mixed races and cultures. And like Saeed, he'd found that it led to confusions as he grew up. What was he – Asian or English? At the interview he was heated on the subject of the 'image' of Asians on television. Warning bells started ringing.

Would he only want his race depicted in a certain way for example? Only sympathetically? Only with dignity? More immediately there was a simple problem of size. Andrew was six feet tall, and Shreela was only five feet three. How could they both be contained in the same shot?

Ross Davidson, a sporty, good-looking, working-class Scot, had all the right qualifications for Debbie's live-in lover, Andy. On an equal footing with his female partner, Andy was meant to

Right: Shreela Ghosh was a late arrival as casting continued through the autumn of 1984. Born in India and educated in England, she grasped the conflicts in the character of Naima Jeffery straightaway, the girl who makes a marriage of convenience which quickly falls apart. Andrew Johnson who played Saeed Jeffery was also born in India and came to England as a young child.

represent newish thinking about the male-role. He had to be piggy-in-the-middle, somewhere between wimp and macho. He had to be a *gentle*-man. Ross himself came over as a bit of a male chauvinist, what would he make of the character's softer qualities?

'Any sign of an Ian yet . . .?'

Matthew Robinson, who had first mentioned Leslie Grantham's name, was very keen for Julia and Tony to meet an actress called Jean Fennell for the part of Angie. As the two of them were slowly warming to the idea of Leslie playing Den, at least when they met possible Angies they had a rough idea of what one half of the tempestuous relationship could be like. Jean was genuine East-end. She had something in her personality that was quite unique, a quality difficult to describe. (As difficult as it would be to pin-point the qualities of a Twiggy or a Lorraine Chase.) She combined vitality with vulnerability, and an almost desperate nervous energy. All of which was perfect for Angie. But did she possess the physical energy as well? Angie was non-stop blood and guts, and would never let up for a second. Jean had a frailness. Above all, of course, Angie was all heart. And that was something that did not entirely come through in Jean's reading of the part. But it was a difficult thing to do, to indicate all the aspects of a person's character, in a short reading of only one scene. One thing was certain, though, she would look terrific paired with Leslie. Perhaps they should hang back? Wait and see if any other candidates turned up for the part. If not, well perhaps they would take a risk and play a long-shot?

'I think we've found an Ian! Some agent's phoned . . . used to know a young lad who gave up the business, left London and went to live in Wales. He's at a butcher's shop, or something. Find him and get him here!'

Ian was fourteen, but had to be played by a sixteen-year-old. Because of Gillian's colouring, they also wanted him to be fair. And because of Gillian's age, he had to look *very* young. Adam Woodyatt arrived from Wales, played 'Happy Families' with Gillian and Peter, and four weeks later was living in 'digs' in Elstree.

Adam Woodyatt who plays Ian Beale began his acting career at the age of twelve and is the youngest of the teenage cast members.

Jonathan Powell asked for a meeting with Julia and Tony. They braced themselves. Obviously he'd read the first six scripts. He didn't have a lot to say. Generally, he thought the show got off to a good start, if a little aggressively. Was it too abrasive? Were too many characters introduced too soon? Would the audience be able to take them all in? Wouldn't they get confused? And was it possibly too fast-moving? 'Bitty' even? Fragmented. But his remarks were questions, not demands. He had a few specific comments to make as well, suggesting odd line changes here and there. Do we need a 'bloody' on page one he would ask, and so on. At the conclusion of the meeting he said, *'Of course you two know more about this sort of programme than I do, so feel free to ignore everything I've said . . .'* This was a new style BBC! They were actually being trusted and allowed to get on with it!

In the autumn of 1986 Julia Smith reflects
on eighteen action-packed months in the
on-screen life of Albert Square and more
than two years of excitement and drama
behind the scenes.

Shortly after Leslie Grantham was offered the part of Den, he telephoned the office and asked to see Julia urgently. When they met he was even more agitated than he had been at the first interview. He said that he had something to tell her that he had not mentioned before because he never believed that he would get the job. As a young man, in the Army in Germany, he had been convicted of the murder of a taxi driver, and had served a long spell in prison. If someone were to discover this fact, or recognise him, the resultant publicity might do enormous damage to the programme and the BBC. Perhaps Julia should withdraw her offer. She didn't. In her opinion, he had paid the full penalty that society requires for a mistake committed in his past, and it was a Christian duty to forgive. The offer still stood. (The bare facts of this meeting were later relayed to Cheryl-Anne Wilson, who had recently been appointed publicity officer for East-enders.)

Before Julia left for Manchester to take up Bill Podmore's invitation to visit the set of 'Coronation Street', she went to look at her own set. Albert Square was almost finished. Standing in the middle of it, at night, was an uncomfortable sensation. It was so real. The pub on the corner, the cafe, the supermarket, the modern flats where the bomb had dropped, the railway-bridge. Yet everything was shut-up, and there were no lights on. No people. No trains. No buses, taxis or cars. Street lamps still had to go in. And British Telecom would be arriving soon to install the red phone box on the corner and the large telegraph pole in the middle of the gardens. As Julia looked, she asked herself: *'Is it all there . . .?'*

In Granada-land, Julia Smith and Bill Podmore were able to talk in more depth than had been possible in Italy. The first thing that struck her about the 'Coronation Street' set-up was its size. There were so many people involved in making the programme. She would remember to tell Tony about the researchers. In fact Tony had already worked out for himself that East-enders was lacking in that area. A single script would often contain up to fifteen different stories, each one needing careful and detailed research. This was something that at present Tony had to do himself, along with all his other duties.

The 'Street' also had its own 'historian' (this was a new one on Julia!) who recorded and cross-indexed every single thing that happened in the programme, and was able to produce that information at the drop of a hat. When was Vera's birthday? for example or how long had Mavis been working at the shop? What was Elsie Tanner's favourite drink? What did so-and-so say to whatsisname in 1966? And what month did he say it, and what day? The mountain of information about incident and character would obviously build, week on week, into a veritable Everest. Obviously a long-running show, and the 'Street' had been running for over twenty-five years!, could not survive without such an archivist. How could the producer, script-editor and writers possibly be expected to carry round all that data in their heads? Julia visited the studios, and went behind the scenes too. The actors had a recreation area (the 'Green Room') and individual cubbyholes, with lock and key. There was a kitchen, and desks where they could sit and answer the avalanche of fan mail in comfort. Julia quickly realised that her programme still had a lot of ground to cover. The visit to Manchester opened her eyes to another thing too. If successful, East-enders would obviously become an industry! It was surely better to face the horror of that thought sooner rather than later. As promised, Boss-lady was taken to the set of 'Coronation Street' and the area where they would be making what would turn out to be 'Albion Market'. She was also shown around the 'Lot' where the exterior set of the 'Sherlock Holmes' series was standing. She had not been completely convinced by the Baker Street location when she saw it on the box. Perhaps by standing in the actual set she might learn the reason why.

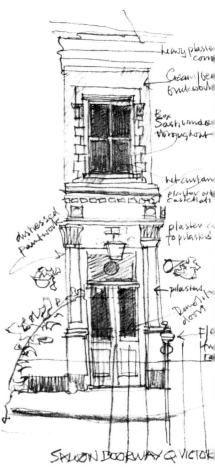

Keith Harris picked up the phone at Elstree. It was Julia calling from Manchester. *'We mustn't have virginal white! Albert Square mustn't look clean! There must be soot and dirt! And – most importantly of all – there must be* **weeds***!'*

The Elstree buildings were almost ready for habitation and staff would be moving out there at the beginning of next month. After calls to agents, and wheels and deals, artists were coming under contract. (And yes, they would go for Jean Fennell.) Albert Square (including recently planted weeds) was ready to receive its first tourists.

These first intruders from the fast receding real world were the script writers. They were like spoilt children playing with a wondrous doll's house, or a model railway. Except in this game the toys were life-size! They found alleyways that they were not expecting. And hidden nooks and crannies they would have to commit to memory for when the ideal scene cried out for just such a setting. One thing they had already got wrong in their finished scripts, was the amount of time it took characters to cross from one side of the square to the other. Scenes with two or more people on the move had been timed to last about two minutes. The actual time was closer to twenty-five seconds!

September, 1984. Michael Grade took up his appointment as Controller, BBC-1, as the East-enders were making their official move to Elstree. Directors and their production teams now had copies of scripts and would put into practice the weekly work pattern that up to then had been only a theory. As predicted, the journey to and from Elstree was a slog, with several working hours being lost, and many tempers getting frayed at the edges. Also, there were complaints about the food in the canteen and the timetable for the 'shuttle' bus service between Elstree and the TV-Centre was a joke. All in all, it was not a promising start to September.

At least the lightweight 'Insert Unit' was ready for trials. But Keith Harris had a new problem. The workmen who had built the low walls around all the Albert Square houses had done too good a job. He wanted them all ripped out, and rebuilt, crooked. Then, as more and more actors (sworn to secrecy about the show) came under contract, so the camera-trials began. The first pictures they produced were excellent, even though the cameras reacted badly to the colour red. 'Get onto Design, Costume and Make-up. No red!'

Then came the revolution! The first three directors asked for a meeting with the producer and the script-editor. With Matthew Robinson, the lead director as spokesperson, they calmly announced that they hated the scripts. They seriously believed that the concept of East-enders was too hard, and furthermore, they had no sympathy for any of the characters. Although they never at any time suggested that the scripts were not real, they still maintained that if the show was to have any chance of success, everything would have to be completely rewritten from the top. Julia and Tony had been carrying this 'baby' around in their heads and hearts for too long to start considering the possibility of a complete re-think. If they did not believe in it now, they never would. The punch had been hard and in the pit of their stomachs they felt sick, but they braved it out. The show would go out as written and there were to be no script changes. Take it or leave it. Matthew decided to leave it. His letter of resignation was received by Julia the next day.

Julia went to her cottage in Dorset for the weekend, to lick her wounds. Fortunately, the two other directors had chosen not to quit the project. Should she move one of them up to the one and two slot, or should she take over the episodes herself? The phone rang. It was Matthew. He was, he said, lunching with friends nearby her cottage, and could he come and see her? Once there, he confessed that he had made a mistake resigning and would like to come back onto the programme.

When he had gone, Julia tried to work out what it was all about, and what she should do. She had always had a good working relationship with him, and he was to turn out to be one of the programme's most successful directors. What was at the root of the problem now? Was it the Julia and Tony working relationship – epecially the 'Tony' part of? Tony would not allow directors to 'tinker' with scripts, and he and Matthew had already crossed swords about it during 'Angels'. Julia had to admit that Matthew was very clever at his job. He got things done, and he got them done in the time permitted. And his visual style could not be faulted. What he could bring to the start of a brand new programme was invaluable. But, if she were to agree to his returning to the show on the strict understanding that no script changes were to be made, what would this do to her working relationship with Tony? Tony was already breathing fire at what he considered to be a massive betrayal on Matthew's part. Surely he would send in a letter of resignation if she were now to do a complete volte-face?

Julia struggled with her conscience during what was left of the weekend and made her decision. Her relationship with Tony had existed long enough to be able to stand the odd knock or two, so she would take the risk that he would not pull out, and reinstate Matthew.

'For the sake of the show' and 'Matthew gets it on' were not good enough for Tony. These were not reasonable arguments at all, just expedient excuses. The bitterest fight they have ever had (to date!) followed, a fight that left a nasty taste in their mouths that they have never been able to remove completely. Making a vow never to allow themselves to be got into such a situation again, they put the whole incident down to experience.

7 September, 1984.

'IT'S COCKNEY STREET!'

These were the words run by *The Star* headlining Geoff Baker's scoop. There was a photograph of him, camera in hand, astride a ladder outside the Elstree perimeter fence, overlooking the 'Lot'. Beside it, an even bigger picture of Albert Square, with the Queen Vic dominating. Their cover was blown. It was to be the first of countless attempts by the popular press to smash down the barriers of secrecy that surround East-enders. It was to be the start of the love-hate relationship between the tabloids and Albert Square.

'What would you say if I asked you to postpone the transmission of East-enders by one month?' Michael Grade was speaking on the phone to Julia Smith. She wondered for a second if anyone else had the courage to make such a suggestion. There was a long pause . . .

'It will cost,' Julia eventually replied.

'Why?'

'Because the scripts have been written so that stories take place in real time. And there are twenty-six of them sitting on a shelf. They will all have to be changed.'

'OK,' said Mr. Grade. *'Nice to talk at last. Anything you want to ask me?'*

'Yes,' said Julia, *'how soon will I know?'*

'Soon.'

Well, he was there on the end of the line, so she may as well risk it.

'I think East-enders should go out on the same days, at the same time, every week.'

'That's taken for granted,' he said.

'Not by BBC planners it isn't!' And Julia continued:

' "Angels" was chopped and changed about from week to week. The audience has got to get used to a pattern.'

In the beginning was the word. The most important part of the whole EastEnders process is the storyline meeting. Here Julia and Tony are discussing with the writing team four episodes that will be shown in four months time.

Right: EastEnders is a continuous production process, a great cycle of hard work and creativity producing two episodes a week, fifty-two weeks a year. Julia Smith meanwhile must keep her eye on future developments, attending to such matters as choosing new wallpaper for the Queen Vic.

Left: The Dagmar came into existence in the summer of 1987 but Julia and Tony began planning for the extension to the Square with its new character and plot opportunities, two years beforehand.

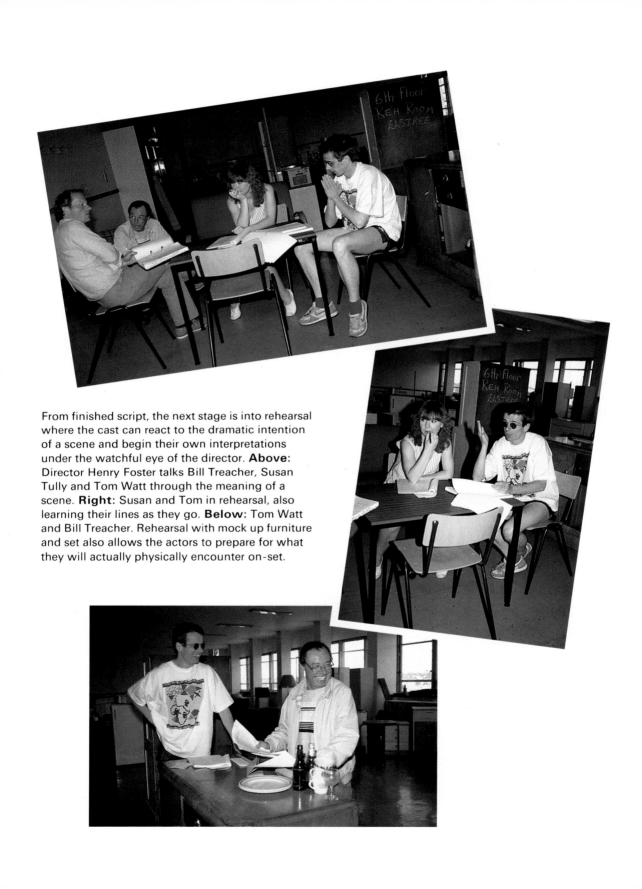

From finished script, the next stage is into rehearsal where the cast can react to the dramatic intention of a scene and begin their own interpretations under the watchful eye of the director. **Above:** Director Henry Foster talks Bill Treacher, Susan Tully and Tom Watt through the meaning of a scene. **Right:** Susan and Tom in rehearsal, also learning their lines as they go. **Below:** Tom Watt and Bill Treacher. Rehearsal with mock up furniture and set also allows the actors to prepare for what they will actually physically encounter on-set.

In the production sequence, shooting outside on the lot comes first, two weeks before the interior scenes are shot. Continuity is very important, for example if it's raining in the outside scenes, it must be seen to be 'wet' a fortnight later in the studio. **Above:** Julia Smith talking to director Tom Kingdon. **Left and below:** Meanwhile wardrobe and make-up are hard at it, getting the cast ready.

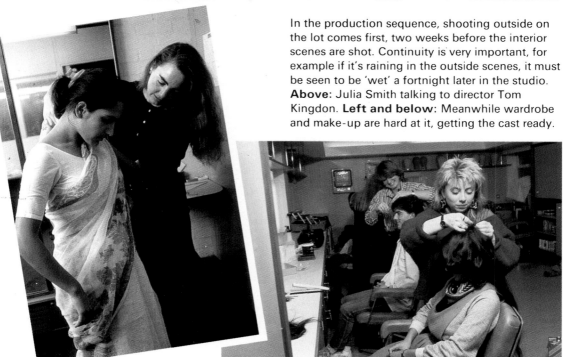

A busy 'lot' day. Behind the scenes of EastEnders is an army of production staff—on any one shoot up to forty people might be involved behind the cameras. **Above:** Director Nick Prosser directing Gillian Taylforth; Nick Berry and Tom Watt in a sunlit Bridge Street.
Right: It's high noon in Albert Square, or rather at the Elstree lot where the director improvises a bit of shade so as to be able to see the camera monitor.

The making of EastEnders requires very fast foot work. The 'Insert Unit' (left) is particularly important, the studio-in-a-van which gives tremendous flexibility both on the lot and in the occasional specially shot sequences away from the Elstree base. **Below:** Ten seconds to adjust eye make-up with a last few quick dabs, with perhaps two minutes before the wrap, the end of shooting … EastEnders is *never* allowed to overrun.

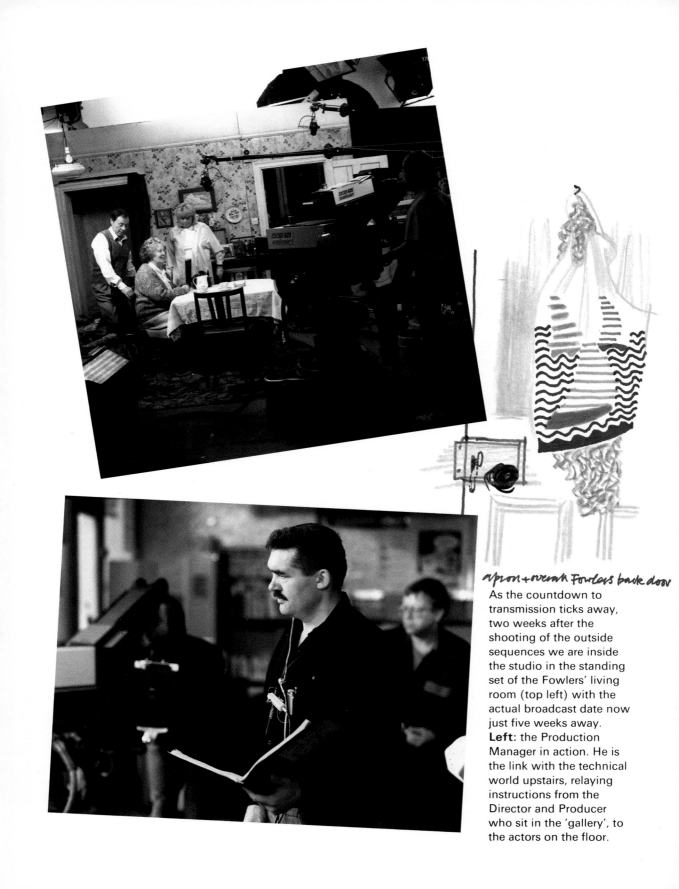

apron + overall Fowlers back door

As the countdown to
transmission ticks away,
two weeks after the
shooting of the outside
sequences we are inside
the studio in the standing
set of the Fowlers' living
room (top left) with the
actual broadcast date now
just five weeks away.
Left: the Production
Manager in action. He is
the link with the technical
world upstairs, relaying
instructions from the
Director and Producer
who sit in the 'gallery', to
the actors on the floor.

The actual recording of EastEnders is done at BBC TV Centre in White City, transmission being made by land line from Elstree. If a line should go down, the whole production process is halted. **Below:** Meanwhile in the gallery the Director is viewing what the audience will actually be seeing on screen in five weeks time.

Breaking the mould—
every so often EastEnders
does something special,
such as the Venice
sequence where the
Den/Angie/Jan triangle
reached its climax.
Shooting in Italy was
particularly traumatic,
union objections caused
problems with a last
minute production
crew switch and, all
the way from
Heathrow to the
island of Torcello, the
cast was pursued by
Press and gawping
tourists. **Above:** This
Orient Express
sequence was
actually shot on a
specially built set at
Elstree.

Was she teaching her grandmother to suck eggs? Mr. Grade said that he understood the problem and would take it on board. Julia decided to chance her arm.

'I want an Omnibus edition at the weekends. Like "Brookside". It means that people who miss an episode during the week can catch up ...' He said he would think about it and would need some costs. He also said he was looking forward to meeting her and goodbye. Understandably, Julia was a little shocked. In the past, Controllers had not made a habit of speaking to mere producers. His answer came soon enough. The transmission was to be delayed by a month. 'Wogan' wasn't ready, and he wanted to launch the two shows at the same time as part of his 'new look'.

So, the scripts were to be rewritten completely after all.

10 October, 1984.

The first press call! This was to introduce the press and the general public to Albert Square, the cast, and at last the title. The actors arrived early at Elstree in dribs and drabs. There was coffee, biscuits and idle conversation, that was really just a front to disguise mounting panic. Had they really got the part? Was the show going to be a success? Were they going to be recognised in Safeway's? Would they all hate each other in a month's time? Remembering each other from the auditions, people broke off into family groups or couples. Julia and Tony introduced those artists who did not already know each other, and tried to put people at their ease. Wendy Richard made straight for the Carmen Rollers and the nearest make-up girl. When she met the press, she was going to look like a million dollars! Maybe it would be the last chance for glamour before Pauline took over her life? No one was quite sure what to expect, which only added to the already highly-charged atmosphere. What press, and how many? Surely, with a cast this size, they would outnumber any journalists and photographers, and this was not even the full cast. At this stage Shreela's contract had not been confirmed, Leonard Fenton was busy with 'Harvey Moon', Ross Davidson had prior commitments, Oscar James was filming, Jean Fennell was ill and Mary was not even cast yet. The tension began to ease as Leslie Grantham and Peter Dean started cracking jokes. Susan Tully and Gillian Somebody-or-other gossiped in a corner. Gretchen Franklin and Anna Wing recollected when they had last met. Andrew Johnson did not know what he had let himself in for. And David Scarboro thought he had landed on Mars! The organiser of the publicity operation arrived out of breath and explained what was about to happen. The artists would all be driven up to the Square in a coach, and there would be a photo-call. Then, over a buffet lunch, and after a speech by Jonathan Powell, it would be the turn of the journalists and the actors would be available to be interviewed.

... We didn't go in the coach. After all, it wasn't really our day, was it ... ? Times like this people don't want to know about producers and script-editors. They want stars! We followed by car, parked and sidled round the outside of the set, the side the audience would never see, until we came to an open space that gave access onto the square. The sight that met us took our breath away. Publicity had erected a huge scaffolding tower facing the Queen Vic, onto which photographers were jam-packed like sardines. The cast was in a long line in front of the tower, all of them gobsmacked as the cameras clicked and clicked ... It had all happened so quickly that they didn't realise what had hit them!

Journalists stood at the base of the tower waiting for the picture bit of the proceedings to be over. They all carried the press handout, which was blue and white, with 'EASTENDERS' printed on.

Jonathan Powell, who had also chosen to arrive by the back way, was as thrown by what he saw as we were. *'You do realise,'* he told us nervously, *'that up to this point, we could have pulled the whole thing ...?'*

The cast was in the middle of a good old-fashioned East-end knees-up for the photographers, when the journalists spotted us standing with Jonathan on the fringes of the crowd, they pounced on us, separated us, demanded tours of the Square, and started their interrogation. What had we done ...? The press wanted to know everything! What was it about? Who was in it? How much did it cost? How was it going to begin? Would it tackle issues? Would it upset Mary Whitehouse? What size audience was it after? What sort of stories would it feature? Was it going to clobber 'Coronation Street'? How long did the BBC plan to keep it going?

That evening, we ended up at Albertine again. It was quiet, which was a relief after the fireworks of a day that seemed to last forever. We had already made the *London Evening Standard,* and in the morning we would be in every newspaper in the country.

10 October 1984 and Fleet Street's finest swarm to capture Britain's first glimpse of the set and cast of EastEnders. It was to be the beginning of a turbulent love-hate relationship between the press and the show.

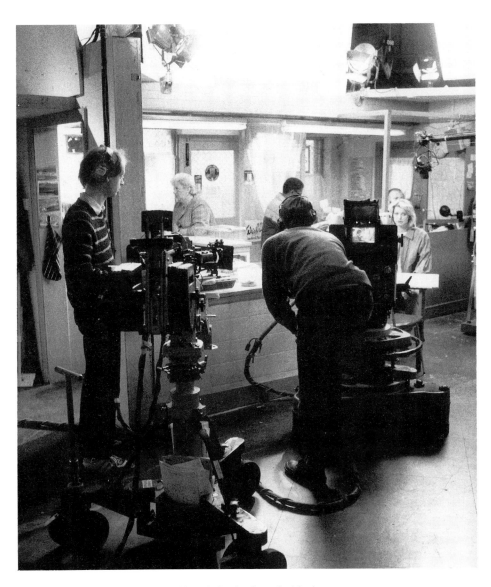

How it looks from behind
the cameras – Gillian
Taylforth rehearses a scene
on the permanent indoor
set of Al's Cafe.

Making it Work

As a result of the first press-call, there was virtually no-one in the country who had not heard of 'Eastenders'. Controller of BBC-2, Graeme McDonald, had found time to read all the newspaper coverage. He kept seeing that title and he knew there was something wrong with it. He sent Michael Grade a note, who sent Jonathan Powell a note, who sent Julia a note. '*What do you think? I reckon the name is right, and I think it should be one word. But wouldn't the "image" of the show be more distinctive if the first two E's were in Caps? EE ... EastEnders ...? Just a suggestion ...*' For which they were to be eternally grateful ...

Now the programme was really working against the clock. Only four months to go before Den was to kick open that door, and find Reg Cox nearly dead. Reg's room, along with all the other studio sets, was almost complete. Casting was finished, apart from 'Mary', 'Nick Cotton' and two dogs, an Alsatian and a Yorkie.

Julia met Michael Grade for the first time. He was surrounded by cigar-smoke, photographs of his family and a battery of television screens. He was in his shirt-sleeves, wore luminous red braces and his blue eyes were every bit as blue as everyone had said they would be. He was one hundred per cent behind the show and wanted it to have the hardest sell possible. Before that first episode went out, every man, woman and child in the land was to be made aware of its existence. Instructions had gone out to all departments. EastEnders was top priority and everyone must pull all the stops out, and back it to the hilt!

Message received, and understood. *Radio Times* was the first to respond to the call. Julia and Tony were invited to the offices in Marylebone High Street for a meeting, followed by 'an informal buffet lunch'. The *Radio Times* Editor's office is actually rather large, but on this occasion appeared to be bursting at the seams. He had gathered together almost his entire staff. Design, Words, Pictures, Features ...

EastEnders was obviously going to be important and going to be around for a long time, so everyone had better meet and start forming good working relationships, so that they could plan an overall strategy. The programme would get the front page, obviously, and what that picture would be was one of the things they were here to discuss. There would be a feature inside the edition, which perhaps Tony ought to write. And there was a suggestion that a large drawing of Albert Square be commissioned for inclusion. And the campaign was not going to end once the show was on the air either. EastEnders was to be a continuing presence in the magazine, with updates on the stories, photo-coverage and articles at regular intervals. The *Radio Times* creative team was not offended when Julia and Tony said they would like a punchy, unstuffy, 'commercial' approach, more like the rival *TV Times*! Dates for photo-calls and interviews would have to be worked out, but what everyone wanted Julia and Tony to know, from the start, was that *Radio Times* was right behind them.

The word had certainly gone out, as department after department took up Michael Grade's challenge with the same enthusiasm as *Radio Times*. As far as publicity and presentation were concerned no expense was to be spared, T-shirts, pens, mugs, theme-music – the full circus! 'Trailing' the show alone would probably eat up three-quarters of the annual budget. Weeks before episode one, there were to be a series of on-screen trailers that would show a snip of the titles and play a few bars of the music. The next week, five-second teasers showing Albert Square for the first time, and 'faces' would be run. Following that, the characters would then start introducing themselves, straight to camera, and explain a bit about what made them tick. They would come on singly at first, then in groups, house by house, building the sequences each week from five seconds to one minute and thirty seconds. ('*Would Tony be free to write the dialogue, please?*') Then, whole chunks from the first two episodes would be trailed not giving away too much of the stories, but with enough included to whet the appetite. And all the time, the 'Albert Square' sign on the garden railings and the theme-music were to be plugged! And EastEnders was to be trailed every week, it was not to start with a bang and then fizzle out. Dates would have to be sorted later for when all the specially-shot material could be fitted into the EastEnders schedule . . . '*But we're right behind you, Julia!*'

There were still four parts still to cast: Nick Cotton, Mary, Prince and Willy, two humans and two canines. In television, dogs that are 'regular' characters are termed actors, not props. But where to get them? The trip to Battersea Dogs' Home was a wasted one. Ethel's 'little Willy' had to be small, and all the dogs they saw there were definitely not. Also they were all much too old to be trained and there was not an Alsatian to be seen. For another thing they were all too dark. The EastEnders dogs had to be light in colour, or they would just blend into the sets and never be seen. Anyway, Battersea Dogs' Home was not allowed to sell animals for use in 'show business'. 'Janimals', a company that specialises in providing and training animals for television and films, called Julia to say they had found a seven-month-old poodle, called Roly, who might still be young enough to be trained. An apricot standard poodle, light in colour, and the same size as an Alsatian.

'How long will it take you to train him?'

'Three weeks.'

He got the part! Prince the Alsatian became Roly the poodle. He was made the property of the BBC, given an I-D card and 'boards' with Julia at her home in London. It was a week before shooting was due to start and there was still no sign of a 'Willy'. 'Yorkies' were thin on the ground. Then Janimals came to the rescue again.

'We've got a little pug ... Lots of experience – he was in "Swallows and Amazons". Any good to you?'

Willy was brought to meet Gretchen Franklin and it was love at first sight.

It was not known at the time that Nick Cotton was to be a semi-regular character, so Julia was not involved in his casting. John Altman was chosen by the directors. Mary, the punk from the North, wasn't needed till round about episode seven, so there was no immediate panic. But as it would make everyone feel more secure knowing there was a complete cast, Julia decided to try and find her anyway. Actresses who had been through drama schools and had their 'equity card' were all too old, so it was back to the letters and photos again. One girl, living in London and doing a part-time office job, looked a possible, and she came from the right part of the country. Her name was Linda Davidson. (Two members of the cast with the surname Dean. Were they now about to get two Davidsons?) At first, it was difficult to imagine Linda looking hard and aggressive, as her face is very soft and pretty. But her reading of Mary was very strong, the accent was

Roly the poodle is a full member of the company. He was cast with less than a week to go before shooting began, in preference to the original requirement which was to be an Alsatian named Prince.

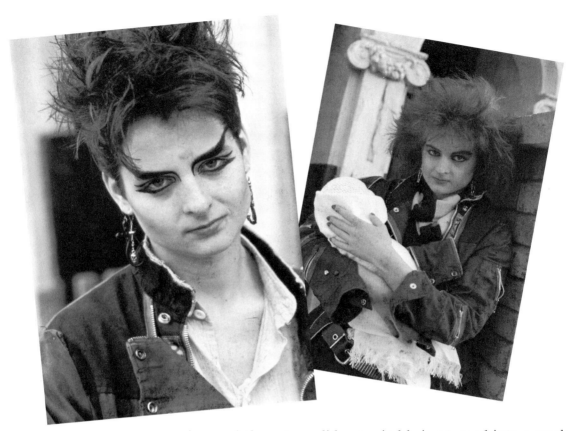

Linda Davidson was cast as the hard, streetwise punk, in spite of her real-life rosy cheeks and red-blonde hair. Mary's make-up has changed through the life of the show as London's street-style has changed.

genuine, and the actress did not mind being turned into a punk. Costume and make-up would just have to take care of the rest! There was, however, one small problem, she did not have a union card. Fortunately for Linda, she had enough experience from her student days, working in cabaret and fringe theatre, to qualify her for membership to Equity so that problem was soon hurdled.

With a full cast and the start of rehearsals just around the corner, it was the right moment for the technical crews to meet the artists they would be working with. A cheap and cheerful lunchtime 'do' was hastily thrown together and Julia and Tony stood back and observed the cast at play. The acting profession is about too many people chasing too few parts. How many jobs had each of them had in the past twelve months? How many of them could afford good clothes, and expensive hairdressers? And, out of all twenty-three (twenty-four now, with Nick Cotton) which ones had the overdrafts? Was all that about to change? At the end of the get-together, they noticed Tom Watt, soon to be Lofty, stuffing the large pockets of his almost floor-length overcoat with sandwiches and sausage rolls.

The publicity-machine, which had gone off the boil a little since the mayhem of the initial launch, was switched on again with a succession of photo-calls (including one for the front cover of *Radio Times*) and radio and television interviews. Costumes had to be selected and given the once over by the creators. Every character was to have his or her own 'look'. *'It's too clean and new-looking. Dirty them up, and break them down. Make everything worn and lived in.' 'Put Lofty in khaki. He's got to look like he's still in uniform ...' 'Ali's got to have a medallion ...' 'Everyone must wear lots of* **gold***. Rings. Bracelets. Watches. Go look down the East-end – they* **all** *do.' 'Sharon ought to look fluffy. Lots of pink.' 'Mary couldn't* **afford** *that jacket!' 'Who got Debs a bikini from Harrods?!' 'No! Kathy makes her* **own** *clothes.'*

The writers met the cast at the 'read-through' for episodes one to six. (Gerry Huxham even managed to turn up on time!) They huddled nervously together as they listened to their words being spoken for the first time by the actors all sitting round one large table. For Tony and Julia it was an opportunity they had not had up to now to test whether or not the storytelling was unfolding properly. Was it carrying one along with it? Was it *hooking* one ... ? Post-mortems after read-throughs are dangerous but necessary. *'Don't let the old ladies pick up each other's pace. And stop them going over the top!' 'Ali needs more fire. More balls.' 'What the hell does Peter Dean think he's doing?' 'The kids are great! I didn't realise their stuff would play so fast. Are the scripts in danger of under-running?' 'Tell Oscar it's telly, not theatre.' 'What's up with Jean Fennell? Nerves ... ?'*

It was a time of 'firsts'. The first day on the 'Lot' was freezing (the cast were soon to ask for the issue of thermal underwear) and it rained. Julia loved the rain, saying it made everything look more 'real'. Geoff Field, the number one cameraman, sat behind his camera, under a huge golfing umbrella, with a permanent smile on his face. 'It's the first new thing I've done in twenty years!' Till then he'd only been allowed to work in the studio. The first ever shot taken on EastEnders was Den running from Reg Cox's house on the corner to fetch Doctor Legg from his surgery. Weather or not, the day-shoot finished on time, with everything 'in the can' that was meant to be. The night-shoot only had three sequences. Angie coming out of The Vic from one door and re-entering it by another. Arthur escorting Pauline home from the pub. And Pete and Kathy manhandling a legless Arthur over to the tower-block. The scene with Angie was postponed until the end of the day's work, because Julia had seen the actress's costume and had kittens on the spot. Jean Fennell was dressed in a full-length black dress with a plunging vee at the back that went all the way down from her shoulder blades to the small of her back. For a Guvnor's lady in a fairly tatty East-end pub (even on her wedding anniversary) the outfit was ludicrous and boss-lady insisted it be changed. It was. But not before a slanging match that was to go down in history between producer, actress and costume-designer where Julia threatened to pull the dress off the actress's back. Even if her back was the only thing the dress wasn't on. First day's work over. And the results looked good.

First rehearsals for the first studio shoot and the vibes were bad. Although producer and script-editor kept out of the way, they knew almost by instinct that something was wrong. There was no feeling of a growing company spirit, no sense of people pulling together and working on a winner. Something was missing What was happening at rehearsals? What were they doing to their show? Unable to bear the suspense any longer, they crept quietly into the rehearsal room one afternoon, and stood on the sidelines watching. Everyone saw them, of course, but carried on working. Matthew was rehearsing a scene upstairs in the pub between Den, Angie and Sharon. He let them run through it once, gave the actors some notes about their performances, then ran the scene again. More notes, then they played the scene a third time. Julia and Tony left the rehearsal room as quietly as they had entered it, and went back to their offices.

Roly jumped up and down a lot when they walked into Julia's office. (He's never quite convinced that Julia means it when she says she'll 'be back soon . . .') But he settled down for a snooze when he saw that they wanted to talk business. Something *was* wrong, that much was now clear. The bad atmosphere had only been a continuation of nagging doubts they had had since the read-through day. Maybe it was even from before that.

Angie, as played by Jean Fennell, did not work. And all their years of experience in the business told them that it never would. Every so often it happens that an actor or actress, no matter how good they are, is wrong for a part. And that was what had happened with Jean Fennell. She had been mis-cast. Not her fault.

Theirs. Try as she had in the rehearsal room, she could not bring Angie to life, because what was in Angie was not in her.

The part would have to be re-cast. If EastEnders was to succeed as a whole, then every separate part of it had to be right. And if a break was to be made it was better, for everyone's sake and for the sake of the show, that the break was made cleanly and quickly.

One of the perks of being a script-editor, is that the buck does not stop at you. It does for producers. Which was why Tony left Julia alone, taking Roly with him. What might follow could prove too much for a young dog's comprehension.

A message had been sent to the rehearsal room that at the end of the day Julia wished to see Matthew Robinson and Jean Fennell, in that order. When Matthew was informed of Julia's decision, he pleaded with her to reconsider. It was early days yet. He would work on the performance day and night till it was perfect. Jean Fennell could get it right, given time. Julia thanked him for his loyalty. But her mind was made up. Angie would be re-cast.

When Jean Fennell walked into Julia's office, Tony had taken Roly for some exercise along the lengthy Elstree corridors. The dividing wall between his office and Julia's was paper-thin and he hadn't the stomach to stay and eavesdrop on what might prove to be an ugly confrontation. But when the noise came, he still heard it. More than two blocks away, Roly barked.

It wasn't a scream. It wasn't a wail. When it happened it was more like a roar of anguish that built in intensity and volume for what seemed to Julia like hours. But the scene was tragic rather than ugly, it was just the noise that made it seem so. If Matthew Robinson had pleaded, Jean Fennell begged to stay with the show. The tears were for real, her words to the effect that Julia could not do this to her. She couldn't. It wasn't human. Julia wasn't human. She'd been out of work for so long. She'd been waiting for *years* for a part like Angie. For a show like EastEnders. For a break. Julia must think what sort of life she'd be sending her back to. She couldn't do it. Of course, Julia always had it in for her, right from the start. It was that black dress, wasn't it? What had she done wrong? What was *wrong* with her Angie? Julia hadn't said a single word about what was wrong with her Angie . . .

Apart from her opening speech, telling the actress that she was being dropped from the show, Julia did not say a single word. She was as poleaxed as Jean Fennell, and wished right there and then that she had become a hairdresser, or a receptionist, or a vet, anything but a television producer. A car had been booked in advance to take the actress home. She left. Julia drove home with Roly. Yes, she did have a conscience and she felt bloody. But as they say, if you wanted to make an omelette you had to break eggs, sometimes heads as well.

It was four days to the first studio recording, and EastEnders didn't have an Angie. Producer, script-editor and directors struggled overnight to come up with some new actresses. By the crack of dawn, when Julia and Tony met at the Shepherds Bush offices, there was a shortlist of two, and they would be coming in to meet the duo mid-morning. But nobody seriously believed for a second that either of them would be right. If they were possibles for the part of 'Angie', why had they not been discovered before? Decisions about whether or not to postpone the first studio recording could not be delayed for much longer. At Elstree, the actors continued to rehearse the scenes that Angie was not involved in. By now, of course, all feelings of company spirit had gone right out of the window, and everyone was privately as nervous as hell. The early and speedy firing of an actress had demonstrated to them all that the people at the top on EastEnders meant business. And if one of their company could be sacked, so could others. Who was next for the chop?

Overnight, the name of an actress had come into Julia's head, but she had dismissed it immediately. As the name refused to go away, she was forced to at least consider it. Julia always thinks back to her teaching days when she's on the lookout for fresh faces and talents. Training would-be performers in the complicated techniques of television acting had given her a plentiful supply of good actors. And a lot of them she had managed to use on her other programmes in the past. Leslie Grantham's appearance on the EastEnders scene had been because of a memory Julia had of once teaching him. And now she remembered another name. Someone who had been at the school at about the same time as Leslie. Julia remembered her as being sharp and brittle, a very 'theatrical' actress, with a vitality that was almost intense and a range of emotions that were alarming, considering her youth. And it was consideration of her youth that had prompted Julia to dismiss her name in the first place. Surely she couldn't be old

The casting of Anita Dobson as Angie happened with just a few days to go to the first studio recording, following a traumatic decision to drop the actress first chosen for the part.

enough to play 'Angie'? Worth having a look at her perhaps? Bit of a long shot, but you never know ... She would inevitably turn out to be quite wrong. Anyway, she probably wasn't available, or interested even ... Julia might not even be able to find her.

But, minutes before those two other possible 'Angies' were due to be interviewed, Julia did find her. She made a call to an agent, discovered that the actress was free, and arranged an appointment to meet her later that same morning. The two others were not right for the part which was as expected. Both highly talented but both quite wrong, they had been suggested out of a desperate panic to find 'someone ... anyone', and it showed.

Anita Dobson arrived just before mid-day for her meeting with Julia and Tony. If she was nervous, it didn't show. During the small-talk that followed, where she and Julia swapped stories of drama-school days and what had happened during the intervening years, they studied her appearance. She was a slim woman, without an ounce of fat on her. Too slim maybe? Her stature gave her a frail, bird-like quality. She looked pale, as if she was getting through the after-effects of a recent cold. Her hair was dark, with a hint of red, and she seemed not to be wearing make-up. She was dressed in a drab, beige raincoat – the sort that Angie wouldn't be seen dead in! – and her smile, which was frequent and large, revealed a perfect set of sparkling white teeth. Her movements were jerky, and she flicked her head from side to side, as if she was already trying to work out where her camera was. But the thing they noticed most of all about her appearance was that she was exactly the right age to play Angie. Also, she was a genuine East-ender. The programme was discussed and the character explained. She studied the audition scene for only a minute or two and then, with Tony playing Den, read for the duo. She didn't speak the words, she spat them. Her Angie was a cat. Or a tigress. Yet the high-pitched, almost melodramatic tone could be instantly replaced by the purr of the kitten. Playful, yet innocent and in constant danger of being hurt. This was the 'Angie' they had wanted all along! It had been worth the wait.

For a short while, Anita's life went on to autopilot, because she had to do in only a few short days what the rest of the cast had had weeks to accomplish. Familiarising herself with the script, costume and make-up meetings, fittings, photo-calls, rehearsals, were all taken at a gallop as was learning the lines for episodes one and two, in which she figured prominently. Shortly before a programme goes into a studio to record, the producer, script-editor and writers attend a final rehearsal, just to check that everything is as it should be. It's called 'The Producer's Run'. Actors are always nervous on such occasions and never more so than at the very first one, particularly when a member of the cast has already been dismissed. But when Julia, Tony, Gerry Huxham (late!) and Jane Hollowood entered the rehearsal-room, they were surprised to find the usual nervous tension was not there. People were relaxed, smiling, joking with each other. Beneath the surface, they were all probably keyed-up ready to bust their springs, but that did not seem to worry them.

Episode One of EastEnders began. Den kicked an imaginary door down, walked into a pretend room and said: *'Stinks in 'ere'.*

Although later they were to give many notes about the run-through and make several suggestions for improvements, basically they were pleased and excited with what they saw. There was a wonderful pace and life about the proceedings, and at several moments they found themselves laughing out loud. By some miracle, Anita was word perfect. And she was so good in a scene in episode two, where Den had to throw her over his shoulder and carry her upstairs to bed, that the entire cast gave her a spontaneous round of applause. But they were *all* almost there. Every single performance was exactly at the stage it ought to be, one day off of a recording. The most amazing thing was the complete turn-around in the general atmosphere. There was a new feeling of confidence and excitement. Getting 'Angie' right had got the company right. For the first time, it was a community.

The studio recording was completed to everyone's satisfaction, as was the videotape-edit and the sound-dub. The treadmill was now in full operation, episodes three and four being already in rehearsal and five and six shooting in Albert Square. And all the time the now established routine of storylining, writers' meetings, reading, rewriting, editing and viewing was up and running. But at least there were two completed shows! Julia and Tony watched them, alone, in fear and dread. But, one hour later, they were elated. It was exactly as they had hoped it would be, everything they had dreamed about since that first visit to the real East-end. But they were all too aware that what worked for them might not for anyone else. Suppose no-one shared their vision? There were two major tests still to come. The reaction of the powers-that-be, and the reaction of the audience.

Jonathan Powell had been asking to see the finished shows for ages. He was used to viewing programmes early on, before a second edit, so that he could chip-in with his six pennyworth. But EastEnders did not have a second edit. And anyway, the duo did not want anyone to see anything until it was exactly the way they wanted it to be. Placing the whole project on their shoulders, and then not interfering, had been a huge gamble for Management to take. Programmes of the scale of EastEnders usually have try-out 'pilot' episodes made first, or even a run of a few episodes on screen, so that people had the chance to gauge whether or not it worked, and come up with quick solutions if it didn't. EastEnders had had none of those things. It had been done cold. The creators had made what they had set out to make, and it was to be greatly hoped by an enormous number of people in the BBC that they had not made an equally enormous cock-up.

Jonathan saw the first two episodes, and was moved to tears. The same day he delivered the cassettes to Michael Grade's home with the remark, '*They've done it!*'

Pandemonium! Episodes five and six went into rehearsals for the studio, as seven and eight were shooting in Albert Square. Another Christmas came and went, this time unnoticed. Proofs of Tony's article for *Radio Times* and the front-cover picture arrived for approval. (Underneath the photograph of the Beale family were the words: **'The EastEnders are here ... and they're luverly!'** Jonathan screamed blue murder and bellowed down the phone to the *Radio Times* Editor: '*Lose those last three words! They're so bloody patronising! I don't care if you've printed* **sixty** *million copies, lose those last three words!*' They did!)

Trailers started going out on screen. It seemed that every time you switched on the telly there was Albert Square, and Jeapes' map and Simon's theme. People were starting to talk about it in the street and there were so many film-crews on the 'Lot', from documentaries, 'trails unit', news and show-biz programmes, that it was beginning to look like London in the rush-hour ...

British Telecom wanted EastEnders to be the first television show to have a 'dial-a-soap' facility, where people who had missed an episode could phone a number and get an instant update. That meant more work for Tony, he would have to write them. ('No more than one minute and twenty-eight seconds per episode, please.') Wendy Richard, in character as Pauline, was chosen to be the voice on the other end of the line ... 'Friday's People' interviewed Julia and Tony on the 'Lot' ... Joan Bakewell interviewed Julia on the 'Lot'. (*Whatever you do, keep a diary*) ... Jonathan showed the first two programmes to the cast at Elstree, and thanked them ... (Wendy came up to Tony, after seeing the episodes and whispered in his ear,

 *'See! I **told** you it was gonna be the bollocks!'*)

At this point they had to stop making the programme, as it was in serious danger of getting in the way of the publicity operation.

12 February, 1985. Sixth-floor suite, the day of the official press-launch. Michael Grade was there, and Jonathan Powell. They were in a small room off the main suite, talking to Julia and Tony. They were drinking designer-water and wishing it was harder stuff. Nerves were barely concealed. Other sixth-floor big-wigs, Bill Cotton, Graeme McDonald, kept materialising from somewhere with messages of good luck. News of Grade and Powell's reaction to the first two programmes had spread round the Corporation like flu, and everyone wanted to demonstrate their support.

In the 'Suite' next door television journalists from all the country's major newspapers and magazines watched the first episode of EastEnders. When they arrived they were serenaded by Simon's theme-tune, and presented with a glossy press-pack, the like of which had never been seen at the BBC before. Suddenly the stuffy old Beeb had gone jazzy and commercial. The contents of the 'pack' told the journalists everything there was to know about EastEnders, even though they would still find at least another hundred questions to ask. As they settled down to watch the second episode, the cast began to arrive in the outer room. Instantly forgetting almost all of their names, Julia and Tony attempted to introduce them to 'ole blue-eyes', Michael Grade. The actors wore blue sweat-shirts (the colour chosen to tie-in with the blue of the River Thames in the opening titles) and their character-names were printed in large white letters on the front.

To build

FOURTH SIDE OF THE SQUARE

possibly the first houses
built in Albert Sq.

Slightly more classic
than Victorian

Design sketches for the
fourth side of the square.
The fourth side completed
in autumn 1986
represented Phase Three of
the extension of the
permanent set allowing
greater flexibility in
shooting.

They stood in a long single-file, family by family, couple by couple, household by household. As the closing music to episode two started, and the lights in the suite were switched back on, Peter Dean opened the main doors, walked to the middle of the room and introduced himself to the large audience. Then he introduced all the others, real names and character names, and they paraded across, one by one, in front of the press. Peter's cockney banter didn't let up for a second … with the introductions over, sliding doors at the other end of the room separated to reveal 'cockney nosh' and the inevitable wine. Then the real business began …

'You're the token black, I suppose?'

'Nick Cotton wouldn't survive ten minutes in the real East-end, would he?'

'Are you trying to get the same size audience as "Coronation Street"?'

'You're the token Asian, I suppose?'

'How long d'you think it'll run?'

'Don't you think all the characters are a bit stereotyped?'

'Why a down-market soap? Why not something glitzy?'

'You're the token Turkish-Cypriot, I suppose?'

'I couldn't have your home phone-number could I . . .?'

'You're the token Jew, I suppose?'

Four hours later the last journalist had gone, and the tables were cleared of leftover bangers 'n' mash and cockles and whelks. That same evening everyone would be able to hear themselves being interviewed on Radio London, Capital and LBC. Tomorrow they'd be in every newspaper alongside pictures of Terry Wogan whose new tri-weekly show had been 'launched' at the same time.

In a few months most of the actors on EastEnders would no longer be surprised to find themselves the subject of newspaper articles every morning, but some of them would be very surprised indeed.

18 February, 1985. By Monday evening, it seemed that Michael Grade's gamble had worked. Every man, woman and child in Britain or so it felt had heard of EastEnders. They knew where it was located, what it looked like and the names of all the characters in it. Julia and Tony would have preferred a softer sell. It had been their wish for the programme to creep quietly into the schedules with the minimum of fuss, certainly not with the brassy fanfares and song and dance of Mr Grade's style. East-Enders had been subjected to one of the biggest publicity-binges ever, certainly a degree of show-biz razzamatazz that was unprecedented in the BBC. But would Michael Grade's gamble pay off? After all that razzle-dazzle, exactly what had Julia and Tony got to show for it? Just one thirty-minute episode, that seemed to be shrinking in stature with every moment. Would those thirty minutes be able to stand up to the hype? There could be no going back – tomorrow they would find out.

The peeling noticeboard outside the Community Centre. The Centre completed in mid 1986 represented Phase Two of the permanent set extension and allowed new storyline set pieces such as 'The Banned' rock group, the jumble sale, nativity play and acted as the polling station in the June 1987 general election sequences.

An aerial photograph of
Albert Square reveals the
great illusion – with
building of the fourth side
still in progress.

The Finished Product

Tuesday, 19 February, 1985. 7.00 pm. Seventeen million people watched the start of EastEnders.That figure would have been seventeen million and two, if the show's creators had not decided to give the programme a miss. It was two years just short of a month since the idea of doing a soap had been put to them. And now that the result of those twenty-three months was on the screen it was the last thing they wanted to watch. They knew it frame by frame, word by word, anyway. They sat in the wine-bar again, the same wine bar close to BBC TV Centre where it had all began, alone. They were tense and conversation was hard in coming.

'It's 7.05. Reg Cox is going off to hospital in an ambulance ...'

'It's ten past. By now they know that Pauline's pregnant ...'

'Eight minutes to go. Lou's going spare about the baby ...'

'Last scene. Nick Cotton's just about to put his fist through the pub window ...'

Just about 7.30 pm, the 'guvnor' of the bar arrived from his upstairs flat with his verdict on the first episode of the programme he'd lived with nearly as long as they had. *'Very good'*, he said. Ten minutes later one of the writers turned up. Bill Lyons, who lived just round the corner. Then Matthew Robinson. They had guessed where Julia and Tony would be. It was the expected anticlimax. The little group talked for half an hour or so, then everyone returned to their homes. Tomorrow was another working day after all. A studio day, reacting to episode one could not be allowed to hold up the conveyor belt of which the on switch had just been thrown.

The following morning some members of the cast appeared on 'Breakfast Time'. The early morning TV show had taken cameras off to a real East-end pub the night before to record people's first impressions of the programme. The 'real' EastEnders were not very impressed: *'The East-end's not like that!' I won't be giving up "Coronation Street".' 'Not bad. I'll be switching on to episode two.'*

The press reaction from the heavies was guarded, from the pops it was mainly good with headlines like –

'Great, Mate!'

'Cockney capers are a hit!'

'Triffic! And full of east end promise!'

'Viewers upset by BBC's soap. Switchboard jammed.'

'Leave it out!'

'Enter the dragon ... Lou Beale!'

It was a slow start. But in less than a few months, for good or ill, no-one would be able to pick a British newspaper without reading something about EastEnders. The obsession began almost immediately. Three days after the transmission of episode one, EastEnders made the front page of a national daily newspaper for the first time. Julia Smith, Leslie Grantham and publicity-officer Cheryl-Anne Wilson had almost been expecting it. For everyone else it came as a bolt from the blue.
The headline read:

'EASTENDERS STAR IS A KILLER.'

The Leslie Grantham saga had started. Suddenly the security gates at the Elstree studios were crowded with journalists and photographers. The devisers were quick to realise that the show's relationship with the popular press was going to be a double-edged thing. Newspaper publicity may sometimes help to boost a soap's position up the ratings. But equally soaps could help to sell newspapers. EastEnders was set not just to help sell newspapers but almost literally to fill them.
One front-page headline had started it off. Within twenty-four hours all the papers wanted, and were determined to get, the story. The BBC put out an official statement that the programme stood by its decision to employ a man once convicted of murder. Leslie Grantham was *hounded* by the press. Subterfuges were hastily improvised to keep him from them. He was smuggled out of the studios by a back route and decoy cars were used to lure the press away from outside his home. All this put an incredible

strain on the actor, and on the show, particularly as it all happened so early in the show's history. But the company rallied round and gave Leslie all the support it could. But the massive press interest in the programme had come as a shock to everyone. Was this just a taste of things to come? Was the public so interested in TV-soaps that it wanted to know about everything, blurring without distinction events on screen *and* the private lives of the stars? Would other skeletons start appearing out of cupboards?

The Leslie Grantham drama quietened down only after weeks and weeks of newspapers trying to wring every last drop out of the story. But it never went away entirely. Nearly every article written about the actor still manages to slip in a reference to his past. Over the months, as a nickname was invented for his character, it was no longer Leslie Grantham who was talked about, it was Dirty Den. Confusions about what was real and what was fiction began. At this point Julia introduced a rule on the programme that no actor was ever to appear in public 'in character'. *'No! Lou Beale can't do a radio-commercial about pensioners' rights. But Anna Wing can!'*

After the seventeen million viewing-figure for the first episode the show took the expected dip to a saner level. Early criticism of the programme centred on its toughness, and speed. Would it ever settle down, people wondered? Had the show found its 'heart', its 'core'? Eventually it did. And as the audience became more familiar with this abrasive little 'baby' so the number of viewers gradually increased in size. Interest was growing, and Julia realised that Bill Podmore's remark about 'your life won't be your own' was becoming more of a fact every day.

The press kept sniffing round the show relentlessly obsessed with any scrap of scandal. Julia was nicknamed 'The Godmother' and portrayed as a ruthless Madame Defarge, who knitted while heads rolled. The actors were photographed wherever they went. Stories about punch-ups in discotheques and 'affairs' within the cast started to appear. Rumours circulated that Julia objected to actors having off-screen romances with each other. It was even suggested that Andy was axed from the programme because Julia disapproved of Ross Davidson's liaison with Shirley Cheriton. In fact several relationships within the company had sprung up by that time and if the producer had sacked all the persons involved then the cast of EastEnders would have been drastically reduced.

Other skeletons did crawl out of cupboards or rather were dragged out by the press, some stories true, others complete lies. One very hurtful aspect was the frequency of headlines about cast members about to be given the sack, resulting in many tearful scenes in Julia's office, where actors had to be calmed down and reassured that the tales weren't true.

The next stage of the press operation was the attempts to predict future storylines, culminating with the autumn bonanza about who was the father of Michelle's baby. The who-dun-it element reached and overtook Agatha Christie proportions. (It was when Den was revealed as being the father that his famous nickname was created.) The programme started to appear in newspaper cartoons as it moved more and more into the public mainstream, one such cartoon showing the Prime Minister telling her Cabinet that the best way to alert the country to the dangers of AIDS was to give the disease to Den. TV impressionists were beginning to latch onto the show's characters as a possible source of material. Tired of trying to predict the nature of future story-lines some members of the press decided to guess, and if necessary invent them! Someone, usually referred to as 'a BBC insider' had blown the story that Den was going to turn out to be gay. (His mistress on the telephone was actually a *man*!) Mary was going to drown her baby. Nick Cotton was going to be pushed off a tower-block. A central character was going to contract AIDS. Arthur was going to commit suicide after first murdering three babies. The male-stripper would turn out to be Den's ex-lover! Sharon would be shown to be Kathy's long-lost adopted daughter. (She would have to be at least twenty-one for this to be possible!)

Whenever press speculations were denied, or failed to materialise, some journalists would say that the programme's producers had deliberately changed the storylines because of what had been reported in the papers! But sometimes newspaper revelations could be uncomfortably accurate. Whole sections of yet to be broadcast scripts were being quoted verbatim. It had to be that somewhere in the company a mole was lurking, feeding the popular press with juicy tit-bits and presumably getting paid for it. Within the production office an obsession with security reached paranoic levels, all scripts were henceforth to be numbered, kept under lock and key and eventually dumped into a large bin marked 'Confidential Waste'. And the big surprise cliffhangers were not

Above: Michelle's on/off wedding to Lofty was a tremendous dramatic hook which enthralled the EastEnder's audience for weeks. On the eve of the wedding, what public and press wanted to know most was what the design of the dress was like and whether Michelle would leave Lofty standing alone at the altar – she did.

Right: Lofty with best man Wicksy. Was he about to become the happiest man in the world?

Below right: Married at last – weeks later they married after all in a registry office.

even to be *printed* in scripts but given to the cast involved at the last minute at the studio recording. People started to eye each other suspiciously. Was anyone to be trusted? False storylines were trailed past certain individuals but to no avail and to this day the mole remains unearthed.

Michelle and Lofty's church wedding was an especially juicy target for press speculation. They wanted to know two things, firstly the design of Michelle's dress, secondly whether or not she would jilt Lofty at the altar. Anticipating an all out press blitz, it was decided to shoot the wedding in a church in private grounds where the press would not have access. They still turned up! In force! Security men were hired to keep eyes and cameras away from the story action. Huge lorries were parked in front of the entrance to the church so that nothing could be seen, and the cast arrived on various odd forms of transport, and in heavy disguise. Finally, strong lights were shone into the faces of the journalists and photographers. They were extremely angry and tried everything to break the security barrier, including hiding in bushes, trying to crawl under vans and even telling the production team

that they were really 'extras' needed inside the church! It was to prove a long day for both actors and press alike. At the end of it, EastEnders had everything in the can that it wanted. The press had to depart empty-handed. Bad tempers cooled down to grins. EastEnders had won this round. There would be plenty of other bouts in this love-hate contest.

One fight that nobody won was one that was totally manufactured by Fleet Street, the so-called 'Battle of the Soaps'. It started hard with cracks about 'rigged' audience figures and the like, anything to set one show against the other. But it soon fizzled out spectacularly. It seemed that there was room on telly for everyone. People working on one soap didn't hate the people working on another. It wasn't a battle at all, just healthy competition.

The stories in EastEnders, sometimes twenty or more of them going on at the same time, were certainly starting to get to the audience. The first big impression was made with the 'cot-death' of Sue and Ali's son, Hassan. The show was praised by audience and press alike for the sensitive and unsensational way this harrowing subject was treated. And people were to switch on for months to come to follow the after-effects of this tragic event. Would Sue and Ali ever be able to have another child of their own? Should they foster? Could they adopt? Would they be allowed?

In a bi-weekly serial it's possible to develop characters over many years. The effects of something that occurs in episode thirty-six can still be felt in episode two hundred and thirty-six, two years later. The revelation that Michelle's baby had been fathered by Den was the next major moment in the serial. It was to be a secret known only to Michelle, Den and eventually Pauline, and the audience! Sharon's story, involving Angie and Doctor Legg, about her wish to go on the 'pill' caused tremendous interest in the country. It was a fairly daring issue to tackle, involving as it did a girl who was under sixteen, and hit the screens at the time when the subject was already on the nation's lips. People started to take sides in the issue: should Sharon go on the pill, or not? Sharon's story became a focus of debate used as a teaching method, both in school classrooms and the home. A large number of families admitted that, as a result of EastEnders, taboo subjects like 'sex' were being openly discussed in the home for the first time in years.

Jan's arrival in the Queen Vic, New Year, 1986, must also be considered one of the highlights in the show's ongoing dramas. For a year she had been someone unseen, just a presence at the end of a telephone. Her invasion of Angie's territory was obviously going to be the springboard for future emotional fireworks.

The birth of Michelle and Den's baby, Vicki, and Michelle and Lofty's eventual marriage helped to consolidate a fast growing audience. Here was a young couple who had come together under enormously difficult circumstances. Were they marrying for the wrong reasons? Would the relationship survive? What would happen if Lofty wanted a child that was their own?

Pauline and Arthur's search for Mark in Southend helped to spotlight the problems some parents have to face when their teenage children disappear from home. Angie's suicide attempt provoked a massive reaction, not all of it favourable. Could the programme be accused of giving ideas to copy-cats? The build-up to Angie's desperate action and its sickening aftermath were intended to demonstrate the full despair of her situation, the horror of it was meant to deter.

Above: Michelle and Lofty celebrate baby Vicki's first on-screen birthday at the end of the May 1987.

Right: Jane Howe as Jan, Den's up-market mistress. For a year Jan had been a powerful off stage presence, the voice at the end of the telephone which jangled Den's and the audience's nerves every time it rang. When Jan actually turned up at The Queen Vic at New Year 1986 it was one of the show's dramatic highlights.

Den and Angie's traumatic two-hander was a risky experiment. A thirty-minute episode with only two people in it had never been attempted in a soap before. Even with a tantalising story, and brilliant writing and acting, would the episode hold up? Press and public were in agreement that it did.

Arthur's story was possibly the riskiest of the lot. His depression at being unemployed was to take place over a lengthy period of time. The deteriorating situation was to be shown head on, with no punches pulled. His eventual breakdown and destruction of Lou's living-room would obviously be harrowing at any time, but especially so on Christmas Day! Would an audience be able to tolerate all that doom and gloom? No matter how good was the quality of the writing and acting, would the extreme depression just be depressing? Den and Angie's divorce and subsequent reconciliation is a very rich and meaty story, but would an audience find it too close to home to be comfortable?

The EastEnders had always been committed to tackling real issues, what could be more real than sensitive subjects like cot-death, depression and suicide attempts? The cot-death for example was a topic on everyone's lips at the time. Julia and Tony knew in advance that it was going to be a controversial storyline, and it was. The real mother of the child who played Hassan was upset and up in arms, and Nejdet had to calm her down as best he could. Because of research done with women who had suffered actual cot-deaths, The British Cot Death Foundation heard about things. Letters and phone-calls started arriving begging the production to reconsider, it was too harrowing a thing to put into a soap-opera. For a while Julia and Tony had second thoughts, they re-read the script, an excellent one from Jane Hollowood. Yes, it could be changed, but should it be? It was a fine piece of drama handled with care and sympathy. They decided to go ahead with the story. Everyone on the show knew how important this whole business was and on the 'Lot' day it seemed that everyone at Elstree had decided to come to Albert Square to watch the shooting.

The opening sequence was Sue and Ali carrying baby Hassan across the Square to the house of Debs and Andy. It was a tautly dramatic sequence and Nejdet and Sandy gave the performances of their lives. Nejdet was carrying a dummy baby, but it was still a harrowing and electric scene. People on the sidelines found that

Bill Treacher as Arthur Fowler, looking pale and gaunt as he receives hospital treatment for his breakdown. It was a tough storyline to explore, for script writers and actor alike but Arthur's story, his prolonged unemployment, depression, petty theft and emotional collapse invoked a tremendous public reaction.

EPISODE 36 by Jane Hollowood

The death of Hassan. A major tragedy in the lives of Sue and Ali, and one that will have repercussions for months ahead, as we follow a cot death through from the post mortem and funeral to the long process of mourning and recovery. In this episode, however we will deal only with the initial shock, bewilderment and disbelief of Day One of the disaster.

We will assume that Ep. 36 takes place the day after Ep. 35. Sue wakes up unusually happy and relaxed after the celebrations of the day before. It is 7.30 a.m. and she has overslept a bit...Usually Hassan wakes them chattering in his cot, but today even he seems to be having a lie in.

She kisses a sleepy Ali, goes to give Hassan his bottle of juice...and immediately sees that he's dead.

She does not touch the baby...is too stunned to do more than croak Ali's name...Ali grabs the baby and shakes it. Utter panic. They haven't a phone and it's too early for Dr Legg, so they race across the square to the only other medical person they know, Andy.

As they hammer on Andy's door, Pauline, getting in the milk, wonders what's up.

Andy and Debs take over. Andy tries to resuscitate the baby (probably knowing it is too late) while Debs phones for an ambulance, Dr Legg and Ali's brother.

She stands shaking like a leaf.
They are all in nightwear except Andy who had been about to go out to work.

The ambulancemen and Dr Legg arrive. The baby is examined...already its body is being shielded from Ali and Sue's view, as if it no longer belonged to them. The baby is pronounced dead. Ali loses his cool, screams at Legg, grabs him, demands that he do something more...that the baby couldn't be dead (he was perfectly alright last night etc)... Ali's two brothers, who have arrived by now, restrain him. Sue, on the other hand is so numb she will do whatever anyone tells her - drinks a cup of tea, stands up, sits down etc. Also her memory's gone...she can't even remember Hassan's date of birth.

The baby is to be taken to the mortuary for the post-mortem. Ali refuses to let it go unles he goes too. He and his brothers go off with the body. Sue is advised to stay behind and for the rest of the day she stays in Debs house, refusing to get dressed, chalk white but never crying, polite and grateful to Debs and Andy, worrying about absurd trivia like "what about the rolls for the pub?" etc.

Debs is out of her depth. Goes off to take her exams. Andy, who has automatically taken the day off, is surprised at this.

Ali returns with his brother and mother. They all crowd into Andy's living room to see Sue. A scene of grief, <u>all in Turkish</u>, with Sue isolated.

they had lumps in their throats and tears in their eyes. If it had this effect on a group of people who knew that it was all make-believe, then what would it do to the audience? Once the episode was edited and dubbed the author was invited in to see it. Jane was very pleased. It had worked, the drama and the sadness mangled the nerves, but the episode had great power.

The Cot Death Foundation meanwhile were getting even more alarmed and approached BBC management to get the episode stopped. Sixth floor viewed the episode, agreed that it was satisfactory for transmission, but thought that the Foundation people should be invited to see the episode before it went out. And that's what happened, though they weren't allowed to do so till the actual day of transmission. At the end of their viewing all their doubts were removed. They thought the story had been handled realistically and with love. Their phone-number was to be flashed up on the screen after the transmission and they provided leaflets and fact sheets in case there was a response for information from the general public. And the general public was waiting for the episode keenly, with its appetite whetted by lurid newspaper reports. The public reaction was amazing. The BBC's switchboard was jammed but practically all of the comments were of praise.

The 'who's the father of Michelle's baby' saga was the who-dun-it of the year, attracting even more attention than the 'who shot JR' episodes in Dallas. A canal location was chosen for the long scene where Michelle gives Den her news. Up to that time it was the longest scene ever done on a soap-opera, lasting all of fifteen minutes. The audience was to be teased first with almost all the male characters in the programme receiving phone-calls and departing the Square in various forms of transport. It was a very cheeky way of opening such an important episode and should guarantee the audience sitting on the edge of its seats.

Roly, the poodle, was the character who finally spilled the beans for the audience. He was seen getting out of the car before there was a shot of Den. Spectators turned up to watch the shooting, not too many, but enough to make everyone worry that the story might leak out. By the time the show got to the Christening of Pauline's baby Martin the spectators had increased tenfold. It was becoming very difficult to record the programme in public places, firstly because of the size of the crowd, but also because of storyline secrets that could get out. On that particular occasion

Writer Jane Hollowood's version of the Episode 36 storyline, which brought the emotional turmoil of Hassan's cot death to the screen.

(45')

66/43 -

S.	Γ	DESCRIPTION
21 cont.		
		MICHELLE turns to DEN
22		CU MICHELLE
23		CU DEN
22 cont.		MICHELL a/b (she turns back to water)
21		2/s
24		Empty shot of water - their eyeline
25		(ACTORS BACK AT CANAL EDGE) Wide shot ROLY - they turn into cam & walk twds it

MICHELLE: (cont) That's not what I meant ... I meant ... no-one knows what happened. What's involved. Who's involved ... They're driving me spare ...

DEN: Who's 'they'?

MICHELLE: All of 'em. Mum, Dad, Gran, Uncle Pete, Kathy ... even Doctor Legg knows.

DEN: Knows what?

MICHELLE: That I'm in the ... that I'm pregnant. And, they're taking it away from me Den that's why I had to talk to you. It's to do with you as well

/(HE CHOOSES NOT TO ANSWER THIS ONE)

They made a list ... all the possible alternatives ... Put ticks on some, crosses on the others ... So bloody clinical! And feelings don't come into it. Oh no Just practical things/... And I wasn't even consulted. No-one was interested in my opinions. It was as if it was nothing to do with me ... I began to feel like ... - a 'problem' that has to be solved. Like a bunged-up sink ... Well, it is to do with me! And I do have opinions ... And feelings .../

(A PAUSE/ FOR AS LONG AS POSSIBLE, WHILE THEY WALK)

DEN: You're sure, are you ...

- 43 -

Pages from the original shooting script of Episode 66 where Michelle tells Den that she is pregnant and that 'It's to do with you as well'. Their secret was shared by the audience but not by Lofty.

Pauline's baby Martin –
scene stealer Number 1!

no one, apart from Julia and Tony, knew what the baby's name was going to be. Just before the sequence was shot, Julia handed a piece of paper to Gillian Taylforth with the name 'Martin' on it.)

The popular press had a field day speculating about the identity of the father of Michelle's baby. What were the odds on Ali? . . . What were the odds on Tony? . . . What were the odds on Den? . . . It even got as far as the betting-shops . . . Hot favourites up to the night of transmission were Ali and Den.

As with the showing of episode one, Julia and Tony decided to give the episode a miss. He had written it and she had directed it and they were both very nervous. Julia worked late at the office and Tony walked home, slowly . . . Half-way home he realised that he had left the office too early. He would still be home in time to watch that scene . . . He stopped at a bus-stop, to waste a few more minutes. As he stood facing the road he noticed the other people in the queue were all facing the opposite direction. He turned round to see what they were looking at. The bus-stop was next to a television rental shop. And there were Den and Michelle playing their scene on fifteen different sets!

Next day the episode was all that people could talk about. And read about too. The press went wild, even the posh papers deciding to comment on the events of the night before on that canal bank. It was at this point that Dennis Watts became 'Dirty Den', and the audience figures started to get out of hand.

It seemed a good time for Julia and Tony to take stock of everything that had happened to the series. Were they staying on course? Were the characters that they'd created in Lanzarote appearing on the screen, or were they getting carried away by success and public interest? They had anticipated that Den and Angie would be popular characters, but they had not guessed just how hysterical the reaction to them would be. Den and Angie would have to be played-down for a while so that other people would have the opportunity to shine through. Of course that would all have to wait for a while because they were already locked into so many stories, Angie's unsuccessful suicide attempt for a kick-off. The actress was nervous of playing the scene and didn't really like the whole story. In the same way that she was unhappy about the whole 'drunk' side to her character.

Playing a character on such an emotional level week in week

out can be very draining on an actress, and it's hardly surprising that at several moments Anita fought the script department for changes. But once she had been sat down and talked through the overall storyline the part became clearer for her, and she agreed to play the scenes. And her performance was brilliant! There was a public outcry about the last two shots of the suicide episode and Julia had one of them cut for the omnibus edition. The build-up to Angie's terrible act and the subsequent following-up of the story was not meant to be sensational, but a lot of people considered it to be so.

It had been decided way in advance that the big New Year cliffhanger would be the killing-off of a character in the best 'soap' tradition. The golden rule of long-running serials is that the person chosen should have the greatest effect on the remaining characters. So who, out of those twenty-four, would most affect the others by being killed? Pete Beale was the obvious choice. His death would leave Kathy a widow and Ian would have to take over as the head of the house. Lou was Pete's mother. Pauline his twin sister. Den his best mate ... And everyone knew him from the fruit and veg stall ... Storylines were planned. Then, at the last minute, Julia got cold feet. His character was a typical East-ender, a solid reliable man, an anchor of normality in a sea of hysteria. Like Pauline he was a lynchpin character. It would just be wrong to lose him.

This landed one hell of a problem on Tony's lap. First week of the New Year had to have a massive storyline and what could be as important as killing off a central character? Brains were racked for days, to no effect. There just wasn't a bigger story than giving Pete a heart attack, then it began to soak into Tony's head just what an impact the character of Den was making.

That telephone in the hallway at the pub kept appearing in front of his eyes, what would happen if the one person who was never meant to be in the show suddenly turned up? Jan, the up-market mistress of Dirty Den, her arrival could affect everyone in the show because everyone drank in the Queen Vic and knew full well the condition of Angie and Den's marriage.

The Den/Angie/Jan triangle was to continue for many months. The climax was the trip to Venice when Angie, convinced that Den had finished with his mistress, was taken there for a second honeymoon, returning to London on the Orient Express. It was an opportunity to open the show up a bit from the confines of Albert Square (a similar experiment had already been tried when Pauline, Arthur and Michelle went to Southend to try and find Mark) and meant that with just three of the show's cast doing two episodes at the same time as the usual two episodes were being done in London, a week would be gained and the cast would get a short holiday at Christmas.

Julia and Tony went to Venice on a recce, with Keith the designer, and the production-associate. The city would certainly provide a beautiful setting for a Den and Angie story. But *what* story? Thirty minutes of Den and Angie on a second honeymoon, no matter how lovely the city, would be just a tourist event and very boring. Tony was not happy, and Julia knew it, so told everyone to leave him alone. Two days later a story was beginning to come into his head, all very vague, but the start of something . . . Something about Venice being a city of Carnival and deception . . . where people wore masks . . .

All sorts of trips had been organised for the final day but the script-editor asked for them to be changed. He wanted to go on a walkabout, and he wanted to see a mask-shop. The masks were all hand-painted and beautiful, and one of them looked a dead-ringer for Angie.

Yes – there was a story here, about disguising true feelings. But there was one thing missing, a surprise. As well as simply being there, something had to happen! Bingo! Den and Angie had to run into someone while they were there, so that their cosy honeymoon would get a bit of edge to it, and who better than Jan, the character almost responsible for them being there in the first place.

Julia and Tony returned from their exploratory mission on the Orient Express and were immediately worried about how much material they would be able to shoot in such cramped conditions. The train itself was not at all what they had expected. There were lots of poseurs and Japanese tourists indulging in silly dressing-up to try and recapture an age of elegance that had gone. They realised that this was yet another form of deception, and so would tie-in with their overall theme.

Union troubles nearly meant cancelling the shooting the night before everyone was due to fly off. The camera crew had to be changed, plus baggage and plane tickets. The Elstree based cameramen were not allowed to go, so the shooting was switched from videotape to film. The first briefing for the film camera and lighting crews was held in Venice with just twenty-four hours to go.

Heathrow was a nightmare! The press spotted Leslie Grantham and he immediately thought the BBC had tipped them off. He arrived in Venice in a foul mood – and Julia had to try and calm him down. This was not an easy thing to do because the press had followed them to Italy. Julia then had to meet two people for the first time, the substitute cameraman and the actor playing Jan's ex-boyfriend who had been cast on the strength of a video.

Pictures of Leslie, Anita, and Jane How were in all the papers the next day. That was that story blown, there was no way that Jan's arrival in Venice in the story could ever be a surprise on screen so everyone just had to go with it. While shooting continued meanwhile, an elaborate game of hide-and-seek was played with the reporters and photographers. They were never told where the next location was going to be, and so only managed to pick up little tit-bits of stories. And it was not just the press! People were

From Bridge Street E20 to the Bridge of Sighs. Den and Angie's trip to Venice turned out to be anything but a second honeymoon.

arriving from all over Italy to watch the EastEnders filming.

On the beautiful little island of Torcello, where Jan was supposed to buy Den lunch, there arrived boatloads of English tourists all with their cameras clicking. Jan actually had to say at one point, *'This is my favourite place in the world. It's so quiet ...'* Leslie's 'nerves' increased, and not just because of the schedule and the fact that he was being pursued by the press. Back in England his wife was about to have a baby.

Very little material was shot on the Orient Express itself. All the dining-car and bar scenes were shot at Elstree in a studio set, and to this day very few people have been able to spot the difference. To simulate the movement of the train technicians pulled pieces of string that were attached to the dining-car tables, so that the fringes on the table-lamps rocked back and forth.

The Venice episodes were completed but had only a moderate success. Perhaps the audience didn't like leaving Albert Square for such a long period of time? Den and Angie then proceeded to take background roles for a while, till their divorce, and eventual reconciliation. Jan faded from the programme she was never meant to be in, and became another of Den's women, soon to be replaced by Mags, then by Angie again.

A strange thing happened to Leslie and Anita after their Christmas-Day divorce. Leslie began to feel very uncomfortable working in the Vic without the actress playing his wife beside him at the bar and Anita, removed from her safe territory, felt the same disruption. It seemed that what was happening to them in the storylines was also happening in real life. The same sort of thing happened to Gretchen Franklin who plays Ethel when she had to give up cleaning the Vic following her hip operation. She really missed the old place. The smile only returned to her face when Den offered her her old job back.

Michelle jilting Lofty at the altar was, like most things, planned ages before, and a nightmare to keep quiet. Her change of heart was a late thought. Julia and Tony realised that since Lanzarote the character of Michelle had had to grow up faster than anyone else. Michelle was becoming a sensible and practical young woman. It was still quite in character for her to have a moment of madness at the church but it was felt that later it would also be right for her to change her mind. The developing relationship between a young couple not 'in love' in the conventional sense, meanwhile

bringing up someone else's love-child, is an interesting one, and one that could not have been anticipated in those far off days. For example, when they first created Michelle, they always thought she would stay the 'spinster' of Albert Square. It was a case of going with the characters, letting the people take Julia and Tony for a walk rather than the other way round.

Worried that the show was starting to get a bit 'soft' a meeting was called with the writers and a decision made to try and recapture some of the programme's original grittiness that seemed to be getting lost in its own success. The character of Pat was introduced to add a new hardness to the atmosphere – and the 'Walford Attacker' storyline was invented. A lot of thought went into the creation of this story because it was anticipated that the show would get a lot of flak if it was too violent. But it *was* violent out there, and real life had to be reflected. It could also act as a warning to people.

Flak was something the show could have done without at that moment as it was already coming under attack for the storyline which depicted Mary drifting into prostitution. Arthur's gradual decline, caused by his unemployment, and the pressures that this put his family under, has been one of the major stories in the

Peter Dean as Pete Beale with Simon 'Wicksy' Wicks played by Nick Berry with Pete's ex-wife Pat Wicks, played by Pam St Clements. They were a late addition to the original cast. Wicksy was invented to bring a character to the show to redress the balance lost when Mark Fowler departed to become a semi-regular. The arrival of the brassy, shrewish Pat, barmaid at the Queen Vic, was the result of a deliberate policy to add an extra edge of toughness to the show.

Early design sketches for the 'extension' viewed down Turpin Road.

series to date. His loss of pride (resulting in theft) and the deterioration of his health was an important thing to take on board. His character had to reach the gutter before he could be put on the straight and narrow again. It was decided that he would not go to prison for stealing the Christmas Club money, until a legal adviser to the programme suggested that EastEnders might be trying to soft pedal. In reality he would probably get twenty-eight days, so that others could be taught a lesson. And that is exactly what happened! At the recording, when the Judge tells Arthur that he's going to prison, the cast opposite Arthur in the dock produced placards suggesting how many years he should be sent down for. Anything to get a smile on Bill Treacher's face – he'd had a very tough two years.

These then were the main story moments hoping to attract and retain a respectably sized audience. Helped by Michael Grade's decision to move the programme's transmission time from 7.00 pm to 7.30 pm it seemed to be working. (This was actually the time that Julia and Tony had wanted right from the beginning. That extra thirty minutes could mean that meals might be out of the way, and more people would have arrived home from work.) It was interesting to find out that the Sunday Omnibus edition

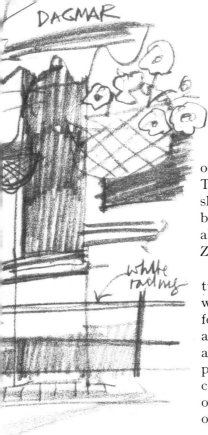

DAGMAR

white railing

...sed area/broken render bricks showing

of the programme attracted a large audience new to the BBC. These were mainly working-class families who would watch the show together first, and then have their mid-day meal. It was becoming a Sunday ritual. And EastEnders was starting to sell abroad. What would they make of Albert Square in Iceland? New Zealand and Australia, yes – but Iceland?

When EastEnders first topped the BBC ratings, Michael Grade turned up at Elstree to congratulate everyone. Perhaps his visit was a little premature because hot on the heels of one success followed another. In what seemed like no time at all EastEnders and the Sunday omnibus edition became the nation's number one and two programmes. 'Coronation Street' was toppled from its perch! It was a 'monster' they'd created, and indeed it had changed their lives. And along with success comes a whole series of new pressures to adjust to. The very fact the show was number one meant that there was only one place to go after that – down.

In the constant search for the programme's 'heart', several 'design faults' had to be ironed out, and that takes a long time in a soap opera where everything is dreamed-up, commissioned and written months in advance. Sometimes it can take up to six months for a change to register on the screen. One of the things that had always appealed to Julia and Tony about the setting of EastEnders was that the community would be a constantly changing one. They had said from the beginning that some characters would have a longer life-span than others.

David Scarboro was the first to go but his departure was not part of the original overall design, as stories intended to run for some time had been planned for the Mark character on the show. But the actor was not happy. He was a young man only part of the way through the process of growing up, and that process was being severely hampered by the day-in day-out slog of making EastEnders. The actors have a punishing six-day-a-week schedule. On the seventh day, apart from crashing out, they also have to learn lines for the following week in the studio. David found that he had no time for himself, or for his friends. Also, the sudden and unfamiliar high-profile exposure that he was subjected to made him wonder if he had seriously wanted to be an actor in the first place. It had all happened so quickly, and he felt as if he had been taken over. It was sensible that David be allowed to leave the show as soon as possible, so that he could be given the opportunity and the space to sort himself out. A break from the frantic round of a bi-weekly drama might help him to decide what he really wanted to do with his life. Maybe he would wish to pursue a career in acting after all, and perhaps he would end up very good at it, time would tell. And if he did opt to be an actor, then Mark could always be brought back into the serial.

The decision to drop Mark presented two immediate problems. One, how was he to be written out? And, two, what would be done with all the scripts on the shelf that he had already been written into? So that the break could be made quickly, the character of Mark was to just disappear. To simply vanish, with no early explanation. Fortunately, the storylining had already indicated an uneasy friendship between Mark and Nick Cotton. It took the minimum of rewriting to give the impression that Mark had run away because he was fearful of Nick, hard drugs and the police. The stories that already existed for Mark were split between Michelle, Kelvin and Ian. It still left a gap though, because several of Mark's functions in the serial, as slightly the eldest of the kids, could not be taken over by the others. A new character would have to be introduced to restore the cast-balance to its original shape. Which was how Wicksy came to be invented.

Happily, David Scarboro has returned to the programme in the character of Mark on several occasions. Like Nick and Charlie Cotton, Mary's dad, Rezaul, Hannah and Cassie, and Dr. Jagget Singh, he has joined the ranks of semi-regular characters.

The character of Simon 'Wicksy' Wicks, Pete's son (or was he?) was thought up overnight. It meant introducing the audience to a character and a story approximately a year before it had been originally intended. Nick Berry, who was already a big fan of the show before his audition, was one of the fastest bits of casting on record. He read for the duo and was offered the part straight away. He couldn't believe it of course, until costume and make-up marched into the room to whip him off for a fitting and an appointment with a new hairstyle.

Shreela Ghosh had to leave the show for a few months to have a baby. In the on-screen story, Naima walked out on Saeed, her husband, after she'd learnt one or two surprising and unsavoury things about his character. On the actress's return to the programme, Naima and Saeed's marriage continued to fall apart. They eventually split and Saeed returned to India. Actor Andrew

Johnson was probably quite happy with this arrangement. He was somewhat disturbed at the prospect of his character displaying simple human weaknesses.

Andy O'Brien was run over while rescuing a young child. And his girlfriend, Debs, married a policeman and moved to Crawley. The two would-be trendies were replaced by smooth-talking Mr James Willmott-Brown, who started as the area manager for the Vic and ended with his own pub, The Dagmar. As old Tom arrived to become the Vic's pot-man, so another household was to forsake the Square, Tony to look for his roots in Trinidad, and his son Kelvin to university. Graphic-designer Colin became the newest contribution to gentrification in Walford, though his more down-to-earth other half, Barry, kept him from getting too rarified. And three new women characters had been added to the Lanzarote list, Dot Cotton, the Bible-thumping hypochondriac and arch-gossip of the washing machines, Pat Wicks, Pete's first wife and Simon's mother, the brassy vicious shrew who's barmaid at the Vic, and Mags, the tough lady from Leeds, running her own catering business, as well as rings round Den.

One or two of the 'departures' from EastEnders sold their stories to the popular press, presumably to cash in on their celebrity and make as much money as an ex-EastEnder as they had when they had been working. The publication of their one-sided confessions (usually containing feeble justifications for being given the chop) have sent only brief tremors of unrest through the remaining company. They were soon forgotten, the harm done being mainly to themselves, as they would not be returning to Albert Square.

New pressures brought fresh surprises. As the show reached a wider and wider audience, so people and organisations wondered if they might be able to use the programme to get over a point or two of their own. Some just wanted to jump on the bandwagon.

While audience-research claimed full credit for the success of the programme, and questions were being asked in Parliament about Angie's suicide attempt and one or two rather disparaging remarks made in the programme about Mrs Thatcher, and a motion was being tabled at the Labour Party Conference calling on Michelle to change her mind about marrying Lofty (Sir Robin Day was not pleased!), so groups of every kind started to flood the EastEnders office with letters. It seemed that just about every minority group, pressure group, charity and commercial company

More late arrivals, Donald Tandy plays Tom, pot-man at the Queen Vic, caretaker at the Community Centre and Arthur's rival in the battle of the allotments. June Brown as Dot Cotton, the lonely lady who spends her life waiting for her Charlie and Nick to turn up, usually regretting it when they do.

in the country wanted to get in on the act. The programme would receive, free of charge, anything from brand new motor cars to pub tills, from glass-washing machines to computer software for graphic-artists. Would the programme please consider featuring schemes for unemployed ex-offenders, self-help groups for single parent families and cures and counselling for alcoholics and their offspring, information about YTS, burglar-alarms for pensioners, hunger strikes for the Third World, International AIDS Day, Community Watch, Steel Band Festivals, organised firework displays, London in Bloom, International No-Smoking Day, telephone cards and the Hospice movement. Every form of illness, disease and revolutionary or unusual medical treatment wanted a place on the show, from MS, cystitis, tinnitus, dyslexia to embryo replacement therapy. (If the programme had acceded to all the requests to include, in all its various forms, the subject of cancer alone, there would not be a single character in Albert Square left alive!) If EastEnders was not afraid to tackle issues, then why couldn't their issues be among them?

Most of the groups got their information to the programme too late, not realising how far in advance the stories were planned. And some expected the show to be distorted beyond recognition, so that their worthy cause could be slotted in. Sometimes, of course, their issues could be worked into EastEnders or were in fact already there. (Julia and Tony do live in the real world and are inclined to know what's going on.) But issues, like everything else in a realistic soap, must come naturally out of the characters and the community. If a programme is to be even halfway accurate, it is bound to fall over issues round every corner without having to hunt them out. Arthur's unemployment is not treated in the programme as a stuck-on 'issue' – it's what would happen to a man like Arthur. Julia and Tony have never liked EastEnders being called 'issue-based'. They don't believe it is. It's about a believable collection of people in a recognisable community behaving as they would in real life.

Teachers and TV programme-makers in the field of 'Media Studies' were very keen on the issue of 'issues'. It started with requests from schools for producer and/or script-editor (or anyone connected with EastEnders!) to give lectures and attend seminars. Apparently EastEnders was doing something in schools. The programme has a large following among young people, and a lot of them would go into the class the day after an EastEnders episode had been shown and talk about the programme and the subjects that were raised, sometimes agreeing with what they had seen, often not. Teachers found that they could use the show as a way of communicating with their students, because it was watched and maybe enjoyed voluntarily in home conditions, unlike the often complex plays the classes were forced to view in the controlled atmosphere of the classroom. Enthusiasm for the programme as a teaching device reached such a pitch, that a teacher from the Inner London Education Authority was eventually seconded to the show for a six-month period, in order to prepare teachers' notes. It is ironic to note that in the light of the handling of the AIDS 'issue' on television, that the only subject that the creative team on EastEnders was expressly forbidden to tackle was VD!

The EastEnders merchandising industry meanwhile was way past the pens, mugs and T-shirts stage. Now there were posters, fan pictures, calendars and annuals churning off the presses and Hugh Miller's novelisations of the show's themes and characters now ran to twelve adult books, tracing the pre-history of Albert Square, and six books specially written for teenagers. The sorting of the actors' fan mail required a separate secretarial staff. The first disc was the EastEnders Sing-Along album produced for the first Christmas. Then Anita Dobson recorded a lyric version of Simon May's theme music and became the first EastEnder to appear on 'Top of the Pops'. Then Nick Berry recorded 'Every Loser Wins' (he was the second to appear on 'Top of the Pops', and his record stayed at number one for three weeks!) and Letitia Dean and Paul J. Medford brought out 'Something Outta Nothing'. Both the latter songs were performed during the programme in an important and complicated story about the ups and downs of a pop group. It was an interesting and major undertaking in the serial but one that Julia and Tony felt never entirely worked. Then Anita Dobson released an album. Then Nick Berry did the same. Oscar James, Peter Dean, Tom Watt, Wendy Richard and June Brown all produced single records. One of the biggest signs of the EastEnder industry was the personal appearance phenomenon which varied from opening supermarkets to switching on the Christmas lights in Oxford Street. The stars of the show are constantly in demand, and if it wasn't for a little

The Dagmar. To emphasise how real life and the screen life of EastEnders is becoming ever more blurred, after the new pub opened, real Londoners were soon ordering a 'Willmott-Brown' in London pubs, a concoction of white wine and orange juice.

thing called 'making EastEnders', they would be at it nightly! In fact, there are now so many requests for them that every one has to be scrutinised and approved by the producer beforehand, so that the smooth running of the recording operation is not affected. But not all the EastEnders stars' personal appearances are for commercial reasons. Their support for charities is constant and sincere with hard work being put in at benefit football matches, hospitals, for Soap-Aid and in campaigns for the homeless and the unemployed. Their first charity appearance as a company was for the BBC's Children-in-Need appeal, an appearance that looks like being repeated annually. Because the cast's appearance at a charity theatre or cinema event such as a Royal Command Film performance guarantees the organisers extensive press coverage, their services are fervently sought after.

One of the greatest moments for the entire production was when HRH The Princess of Wales asked to visit Albert Square. She had met Julia at the Women-of-the-Year lunch earlier in the week, and spoke enthusiastically about EastEnders. Her visit, involving yet another massive security operation to keep the press away from an essentially private occasion, lasted several hours. HRH visited the set and was introduced to the cast, and members of the production team. The programme was shooting a Christmas party for all the kids in the community-centre and the Princess offered her own 'mob' as extras. Later she visited the studios.

Standing in the Queen Vic she said: *'This is what I miss. I haven't been in a pub for years . . .'.*

And then the awards started coming in. As predicted, they were not of the posh variety. Bill Treacher's wonderful performance as Arthur was not even nominated for a BAFTA! Instead of the usual incestuous accolades doled out by the profession to the profession, they were tributes from the people, ordinary punters who sit at home and watch the show week in week out and feel a need to say 'well done' and 'thank you'. To receive a spontaneous response like an award from the public you are trying so hard to communicate with, is the greatest honour of them all. It makes all the hard work, the dramas, the emergencies and the ups and downs worth it, and gives makers of popular programmes the confidence to carry on. On EastEnders, how the large and loyal audience reacts is the most important consideration of all.

All the time Julia and Tony have to tell themselves that East-Enders is not really about T-shirts and hit records. It's not about Dirty Den (who doesn't exist) opening a new nightclub. It's about whether Den will get back with Angie. Whether Lofty and Michelle will have another baby. Whether Kathy's daughter will turn up in Albert Square. Whether or not to kill someone off for the New Year 1987 cliffhanger . . .

The characters sketched in at Lanzarote have changed, as people always do. Lou's health is a worry. Michelle is adult enough to realise that she may have made a mistake in getting married. Sue and Ali are to be parents again. Mary has finally found a friend, and may even be able to get herself together. Colin and Barry, basically single people, are finding the strains of their relationship too much to cope with.

Lofty is now desperate for a child of his own, but what will his reaction to little Vicki be if that should happen? Ian has now grown up, but is he too young for a one-to-one relationship?

Are Den and Angie back together? Will they remarry? If they do, how long will it take them to drift back into their usual routine? Everyone knows what Den and Angie are like, how long can she stay off the bottle? How long can he stay away from the ladies . . .?

In these post-AIDS days Albert Square seems to be going back to concepts of family and couples, or people alone. As producer

Right: Full circle – Julia Smith and Tony Holland with some of their favourite awards won by the show to date, the Stars Organisation for Spastics Award, the Variety Club of Great Britain Award to the entire cast and production team as the BBC TV Personality of the Year and the Television and Radio Industries Club Top BBC TV Programme Award.

and script-editor of EastEnders, we are also changing. As we get to know more about these people we've created (and we *still* read those biographies once a week) we realise how far they have moved on since they were a gleam in our eyes on that Spanish island. Our greatest worry is that one day we will dry-up on ideas. As we get more tired perhaps, or more pressurised.

So far that is not happening. There are a lot of stories out there in the real world and the characters seem to be rich enough to carry story-strands on in a weave that will become more and more interesting. There are still plenty of big stories to come, lots of fireworks we have kept up our sleeves!

One thing you can guarantee with EastEnders is that it won't be cosy. It's always going to be in the thick of things, having a go, and probably shocking a few people along the way. But there will be joys as well as shocks.

Right now we have a large and loyal audience who seem to be telling us that we are getting it right. If they start deserting us because we're getting it wrong then we both hope that the BBC has the courage to take the show off ... Be a funny old world without Albert Square ...

C O N T I N U I T Y : Three Years in the Life of EastEnders

O F F S C R E E N O N S C R E E N

	OFF SCREEN	ON SCREEN
1984		
5th Oct	READ THROUGH — FIRST SIX EPISODES	
10th Oct	PRESS CALL — EASTENDERS	
22nd Nov	1ST ON SCREEN PROMO TRAIL	
1985		
12th Feb	PRESS LAUNCH	
19th Feb	1ST TRANSMISSION	*Ep 1* Reg Cox found dead
5th March		*Ep 5* Mary and Annie arrive in square
10th March		*Ep 10* Debs and Andy 1st appearance
18th April		*Ep 18* Mark's disappearance discovered
7th May		*Ep 23* Mary's father finds his daughter
13th June		*Ep 34* Meet Mehmet, Ali's beautiful brother
20th June		*Ep 36* Cot Death
4th July		*Ep 40* Dot's 1st Appearance
18th July		*Ep 44* Naima has hair cut
1st August		*Ep 48* Pauline's baby born
12th Sept		*Ep 60* Michelle tells Lou she's pregnant
27th Sept	1ST TX NEW ZEALAND	
3rd Oct		*Ep 66* Michelle tells Den he's the father of her baby
8th Oct		*Ep 67* Wicksy arrives in Albert Square
24th Oct	NO I TV RATING	
29th Oct		*Ep 73* Martin is christened
7th Nov		*Ep 76* Ladies' night at the Vic — Male Stripper

OFF SCREEN   ON SCREEN

	OFF SCREEN	ON SCREEN
12th Nov		*Ep 77* Kathy tells Pete about the rape
19–21 Nov	ON LOCATION – SOUTHEND	
21st Nov		*Ep 80* Ian wins boxing match
26th Dec		*Ep 90* Saeed leaves the square
31st Dec		*Ep 91* The Fowlers look for Mark in Southend
1986 2nd Jan		*Ep 92* The Fowlers find Mark
24th Jan	1ST AWARD – ANNA SCHER THEATRE FAVOURITE PROGRAMME	
30th Jan		*Ep 100* Jan arrives at Vic – during drag show
19th Feb	TRIC AWARD – TOP BBC TV PROGRAMME	
27th Feb		*Ep 108* Angie attempts suicide
20th March		*Ep 114* James Willmott-Brown first appearance
8th April		*Ep 119* Michelle agrees to marry Lofty
19th May	PYE AWARDS – ANITA DOBSON: OUTSTANDING FEMALE PERSONALITY – LESLIE GRANTHAM: OUTSTANDING MALE PERSONALITY	
27th May		*Ep 133* Vicki is born
5th June		*Ep 136* Carmel 1st appearance
12th June		*Ep 138* Pat Wicks arrives in square
17th June		*Ep 139* Pat says Wicksy isn't Pete's son

OFF SCREEN   ON SCREEN

	OFF SCREEN	ON SCREEN
27th July	SOAP AID AT ST HELENS	
1st Aug	'ANYONE CAN FALL IN LOVE' RELEASED – ANITA DOBSON	
5th Aug		*Ep 153* Colin's first appearance
14th Aug		*Ep 156* Andy dies saving a child
28th Aug		*Ep 160* Andy's funeral
18th Sept		*Ep 166* Pauline wins Glamorous Granny Competition
18th Sept		*Ep 166* Arthur reveals robbery
20–28 Sept	ON LOCATION – VENICE	
22nd Sept	1st VIDEO RELEASED – 'EASTENDERS – THE QUEEN VIC'	
22nd Sept	'EVERY LOSER WINS' RELEASED – NICK BERRY	
23rd Sept		*Ep 167* Lofty and Michelle's Stag and Hen night
25th Sept		*Ep 168* Michelle gets to the church door
30th Sept		*Ep 169* Lofty is left at the altar
6th Oct	'SOMETHING OUTA NOTHING' RELEASED – LETITIA DEAN AND PAUL J. MEDFORD	
14th Oct	'EVERY LOSER WINS' NO I (HELD THREE WEEKS)	
16th Oct		*Ep 174* Angie tells Den she's dying – first two-hander
31st Oct	HRH PRINCESS OF WALES VISITS EASTENDERS AT ELSTREE	
13th Nov		*Ep 182* Arthur is arrested

OFF SCREEN ON SCREEN

	OFF SCREEN	ON SCREEN
14th Nov	'JUST ANOTHER DAY' TX ON EASTENDERS	
13th Nov		*Ep 183* Enter Barry
18th & 20th Nov		*Ep 183 & 184* Den, Angie and Jan in Venice
25th Nov		*Ep 185* Lofty and Michelle are married and Angie spills the beans on the Orient Express
28th Nov	ROYAL VARIETY PERFORMANCE FOR EASTENDERS CAST	
8th Dec	1st TX HOLLAND	
25th Dec	TWO EPISODES ON XMAS DAY. HIGHEST RECORDED VIEWING FIGURES EVER TO DATE. PT 1: 29.55m PT 2: 31.15m	
25th Dec		*Ep 194a* Den gives Angie divorce papers Angie and Sharon walk out of Queen Vic
		Ep 194b Arthur breaks up Fowler household
1987		
5th Jan	1st TX AUSTRALIA	
15th Jan		*Ep 200* Arthur goes to hospital
3rd Feb	VARIETY CLUB AWARD — ENTIRE CAST AND TEAM: 'BBC PERSONALITY OF THE YEAR' AWARD GIVING	
17th Feb		*Ep 209* Albert Square natural justice catches up with Mehmet
19th Feb		*Ep 210* Pat caught by Walford Attacker

OFF SCREEN ON SCREEN

	OFF SCREEN	ON SCREEN
19th Feb	SECOND BIRTHDAY	
26th Feb		*Ep 212* Jan leaves Vic
2nd April		*Ep 222* Barry's 21st and ramifications!
7th April	TRIC AWARDS: SIMON MAY, BEST TV THEME MUSIC	
14th April	IVOR NOVELLO AWARDS FOR BEST-SELLING A-SIDE RECORD – 'EVERY LOSER WINS'	
15th April		*Ep 225* Walford Attacker caught
27th April	1ST TX: NORWAY	
28th April		*Ep 229* Arthur comes home from hospital
5th May		*Ep 231* Mags arrives as Den's new date
7th May		*Ep 232* Arthur's trial
14th May		*Ep 234* Debs and Rich: engagement party
14th May		*Ep 234* Mary's parents take Annie
17th May	S.O.S. STAR AWARDS FOR FAVOURITE TV PROGRAMME	
26th May		*Ep 237* Den and Jan's last meeting
28th May		*Ep 238* Tony goes home to Caribbean
11th June		*Ep 242* Election Day – the EastEnders vote
18th June		*Ep 244* Lofty's Aunty Irene dies
25th June		*Ep 246* The Dagmar re-opens
26th June	TONY BLACKBURN – RADIO LONDON BROADCAST FROM ELSTREE	
30th June	1ST TX BARCELONA DUBBED INTO CATALAN	

OFF	SCREEN	ON	SCREEN

2nd July		Ep 248	Dot and Ethel – second two-hander
9th July	ANNOUNCEMENT PROGRAMME SOLD TO PBS STATIONS IN AMERICA		
28th July		Ep 255	Darren arrives; Carmel moves into square
6th Aug		Ep 258	Den sacks Wicksy
20th Aug		Ep 262	Dagmar v Queen Vic five-a-side football
3rd Sept		Ep 266	Kelvin leaves for University
1st Oct		Ep 274	Den and Angie – fireworks!!
20th Oct		Ep 279	Sue announces that she's pregnant – at last

PICTURE CREDITS

BBC © vi, 5, 25, 28, 31, 32, 34, 37, 40, 41, 65, 66, 67, 68, 69, 70, 71, 72, 95, 104, 105, 106, 107, 108, 109, 110, 111, 112, 113, 114, 121, 124, 131, 135, 137, 144, 147, 148, 149, 150, 151, 152, 153, 156–7, 158, 164, 169, 177, 184, 185, 187, 188, 193, 194, 197, 199, 203, 209. Keith Harris 15, 37 (top). Julia Smith 40, 41. Sunday Mirror (Geoff Wilkinson) 138–9, 163. Aerofilms Ltd 178.

Line drawings throughout are by Keith Harris, except those on 51, 52, 54, 55, 56, 59, 63 by Sue Rawkins.